BEYOND THE CLOUDS: THE DAILY DEVOTIONAL WORKBOOK FOR TEEN GIRLS:

PRAYERS, TECHNIQUES, AND EXERCISES TO HELP MANAGE YOUR ANXIETY AND STRESS IN ONLY 11 WEEKS

BIBLICAL TEACHINGS

Copyright © 2023 by Biblical Teachings - All rights reserved.

No part of this book may be reproduced in any form or by any electronic or mechanical means, including information storage and retrieval systems, without written permission from the author, except for the use of brief quotations in a book review.

Under no circumstances will any blame or legal responsibility be held against the publisher, or author, for any damages, reparation, or monetary loss due to the information contained within this book, either directly or indirectly.

Legal Notice:

This book is copyright protected. It is only for personal use. You cannot amend, distribute, sell, use, quote, or paraphrase any part, or the content within this book, without the author or publisher's permission.

Disclaimer Notice:

Please note that the information contained within this document is for educational and entertainment purposes only. All effort has been executed to present accurate, up-to-date, reliable, complete information. No warranties of any kind are declared or implied. Readers acknowledge that the author is not rendering legal, financial, medical, or professional advice. The content within this book has been derived from various sources. Please consult a licensed professional before attempting any techniques outlined in this book.

By reading this document, the reader agrees that under no circumstances is the author responsible for any losses, direct or indirect, that are incurred due to the use of the information in this document, including, but not limited to, errors, omissions, or inaccuracies.

CONTENTS

Your First Step Toward a Calm Mind   vii

1. Technique Spotlight: The 5-4-3-2-1 Method   1
2. What's Anxiety & Stress?   3
3. Causes of Anxiety & Stress   5
4. The Power of Thoughts   7
5. Faith, Anxiety, and Stress - Oh My!   9
6. Technique Spotlight: Body Scan   12
7. School   14
8. Relationships   16
9. Social Media   18
10. Health   20
11. Technique Spotlight: Relaxation Techniques   24
12. Deep Breathing   26
13. Progressive Muscle Relaxation   28
14. Visualization   30
15. Mindfulness Meditation   32
16. Technique Spotlight: Gratitude Journaling   36
17. Exercise and Fitness   38
18. Healthy Eating & Drinking   40
19. Good Sleep Hygiene   42
20. Limiting Screen Time   44
21. Technique Spotlight: Evaluating Priorities   48
22. Facing the Fear of Failure   51
23. The Importance of Planning   53
24. Celebrating Small Wins   55
25. Overcoming Procrastination   57
26. Technique Spotlight: Hugging   60
27. Identifying Supportive People   62
28. Communication in Relationships   64
29. Setting Boundaries   66
30. Building New Connections   68
31. Technique Spotlight: A.A.S.P - Anxiety Attack Safety Plan   72

32. The Power of Facing Your Fears	75
33. Visualize Success	77
34. Start Small	79
35. Celebrating Progress	81
36. Technique Spotlight: Brain Dump	84
37. Coping Through Visual Art	86
38. The Therapeutic Power of Writing	88
39. Listening to Music as a Calming Tool	90
40. Time Management	92
41. Technique Spotlight: Prayer	96
42. The Power of Prayer	98
43. Finding Comfort in Scripture	100
44. Community and Fellowship	102
45. Hope & Trust in God	104
46. Technique: Practicing Self-Care	108
47. Unplug and Disconnect	110
48. Engage in Hobbies & Creative Activities	112
49. Have a Mental Health Day	114
50. Say No to Things That Drain You	116
51. Technique Spotlight: Embrace What Resonates	120
52. Reflecting on Progress	123
53. Learning from Setbacks	125
54. Embracing Change	127
55. Moving Forward with Confidence	129
Walking Forward with Peace	131

BIBLE STUDY
-Starter Kit-

Discover a **Simple**, **Powerful** Way to Study **The Bible**

- *No More Guesswork* - Learn to Explore the Bible **with Confidence** and Clarity.

- Discover a Study Method That *Fits Seamlessly into Your Busy Life* - **Without the Overwhelm**.

- **Build a Bible Study Routine** *You'll Actually Look Forward To* - Not Just Another Task on Your To-Do List.

SCAN THE QR CODE FOR YOUR FREE COPY

YOUR FIRST STEP TOWARD A CALM MIND

SCAN ME

You're taking your first step in an exciting journey to tackle stress and anxiety with real-life help from the Bible. Seriously, that's so brave and amazing of you! Life as a teen can be overwhelming—school, friends, family, and just trying to figure out who you are. It's a lot to juggle, and feeling anxious or stressed sometimes is totally normal. But this devotional workbook is here to help you through it.

This book was made with you in mind—for the ups and downs you face every day. I hope what's inside these pages speaks to your heart and gives you the encouragement you need. Each chapter is filled with tools, wisdom, and support straight from God's Word to help you find strength, peace, and joy—even when life feels like a whirlwind.

Oh, and here's something fun: each week includes beautifully illustrated coloring pages designed just for you. These aren't just for fun— they're a way to relax, reflect, and express yourself while working through each chapter. Grab some colored pencils or markers and make these pages your own!

How to Use This Book

Over the next 11 weeks, you'll learn practical ways to handle stress and anxiety while deepening your connection to God.

Here's what to expect each week:

1. **Technique Spotlight:** Start with a tool or method to help tackle stress.
2. **Read the Devotions:** Each devotion dives into a specific theme, combining real-life wisdom with God's Word. They're short and easy to read, making them perfect for busy days.
3. **Reflection Prompts:** Answer these prompts in a journal, talk them over with a trusted friend, or simply take time to think them through.
4. **Prayer:** Wrap up each devotion with a moment of prayer. Use the prayer in the book or talk to God in your own words—He's always listening and loves hearing from you.
5. **Color and Relax:** Dive into the coloring pages anytime—to start your week, take a break, or unwind while reflecting on what you've learned. Get creative!

Stick with it, and by the end of these 11 weeks, you'll have a better understanding of your stress triggers, awesome coping strategies, and a toolkit of techniques to handle life's challenges. You'll feel more confident, balanced, and ready to take on anything.

A Quick Note

If your stress or anxiety ever feels too big to handle alone, it's okay to reach out for extra support. Talking to a therapist, counselor, or someone you trust can make a huge difference. This workbook is a great start, but sometimes we all need a little extra help—and that's totally normal.

Stay Connected!

If you'd like to stay in touch and keep the good vibes going, scan the QR code at the top of this page to join our Facebook community. It's a space for connection, encouragement, and growth, where you'll meet other teens walking the same journey.

You've got this—and God's got you! Let's dive into this adventure together.

P.S. All scripture quotations are taken from the Holy Bible, New International Version (NIV), unless otherwise noted.

Week 1

Understanding Anxiety & Stress

1
TECHNIQUE SPOTLIGHT: THE 5-4-3-2-1 METHOD

___ /___ / _____

The 5-4-3-2-1 Method

The 5-4-3-2-1 (or the 5 senses) method is a grounding technique that can help you manage stress and anxiety by focusing on your immediate surroundings. It involves using the five senses to bring attention to the present moment and create a sense of calm.

Here's a step-by-step example of the exercise:

1. Find a comfortable place to sit or stand and take a few deep breaths to center yourself.
2. Look around and identify 5 things that you can see. It could be anything from a chair to a picture on the wall.
3. Next, identify 4 things that you can touch. You could run your fingers along the surface of a table or feel the texture of a piece of clothing.
4. Then, identify 3 things that you can hear. It could be the sound of birds chirping outside, the hum of a fan, or the sound of your own breath.

5. Next, identify 2 things that you can smell. It could be the scent of flowers, the smell of fresh laundry, or a familiar scent that you associate with a positive memory.
6. Finally, identify 1 thing that you can taste. This could be a sip of water or tea, a piece of gum, or a small snack.

By focusing on the five senses, this exercise will help you to shift your attention away from anxious or stressful thoughts and bring your focus to the present moment. It can also help to create a sense of relaxation and calmness.

How did focusing on your five senses make you feel in the moment?

Did this exercise help you feel calmer or more present? Why or why not?

_____

_____

_____

_____

_____

_____

_____

_____

_____

_____

_____

_____

_____

2
WHAT'S ANXIETY & STRESS?

___ /___ / _____

"Do not be anxious about anything, but in every situation, by prayer and petition, with thanksgiving, present your requests to God."

— PHILIPPIANS 4:6

You know what it feels like when the pressure is on. Your heart races, your palms sweat, and your nervous thoughts seem louder than anything else. Maybe it's before a big game, a test, or even a conversation you've been dreading. That's exactly what happened to Ava.

Ava started to notice her hands shaking before every match. The expectations from her coach, teammates, and even herself weighed heavily on her. It made her feel anxious and stressed, and she began to wonder if she could handle it at all.

When her mom noticed how tense Ava was, she stepped in to help. She explained that anxiety is when you feel fear, worry, or unease, and stress is how your body reacts to big challenges. These feelings aren't unusual, but if they build up, they can affect your mood, body, and even your relationships.

Here's the good news: You don't have to face anxiety or stress alone. Ava's mom shared some helpful tools, like deep breathing, journaling, and talking to someone you trust. More importantly, Ava learned to pray when she felt overwhelmed, giving her worries to God. Over time, these small steps made a big difference. Ava started feeling more confident, both on and off the field.

You might feel like Ava sometimes. Life can get overwhelming, and it's easy to feel like you're carrying it all on your own. But remember, God invites you to bring your worries to Him. He wants you to trust Him with the things that make your heart race and your thoughts spin. And just like Ava, you can take practical steps to manage your stress and grow stronger each day.

Your Turn

Think about a time when you felt anxious or stressed. What triggered those feelings? Write about how you handled it and what you might do differently next time.

Describe what helps you feel calm and grounded when you're feeling overwhelmed. Is it prayer, deep breathing, or something else?

Prayer

Dear God, thank You for being a steady presence when life feels overwhelming. Help me to trust You with my worries and fears. Teach me to rely on Your peace and to take practical steps to manage stress and anxiety. Amen.

3
CAUSES OF ANXIETY & STRESS

___ / ___ / _____

"Come to me, all you who are weary and burdened, and I will give you rest."

— MATTHEW 11:28

Ashley, a high school student, was feeling overwhelmed by everything on her plate. Between her part-time job, extracurricular activities, and a demanding course load, she struggled to keep up. The constant pressure to balance it all left her feeling anxious and stressed, and she started to experience physical symptoms like headaches and stomachaches.

One day, Ashley confided in her friend Bella, who suggested they talk to the school counselor. The counselor explained that Ashley's symptoms were caused by stress and anxiety, which can come from a variety of sources. Sometimes, people are naturally predisposed to stress due to genetics. Other times, life events or environmental factors contribute to those feelings.

The counselor emphasized the importance of understanding the root cause of anxiety and stress to manage them effectively. With this knowledge, Ashley started taking steps to address her feelings. She learned that she didn't have to face her struggles alone. Talking to a trusted adult and leaning on her faith reminded her that God cares deeply for her and wants her to cast her worries on Him.

Ashley's story highlights how important it is to identify the source of stress and anxiety. Recognizing these causes can lead to healthier ways of coping and more effective strategies to feel at peace. God invites everyone to come to Him when they feel burdened, offering comfort and rest for even the heaviest of hearts.

Your Turn

What activities or situations in your life make you feel overwhelmed? Write about one and think of ways you could approach it differently.

Imagine sharing advice with someone else who feels stressed. What would you say to help them?

Prayer

Dear God, thank You for reminding us that we don't have to carry our burdens alone. Help us to identify the root causes of our anxiety and stress so we can manage them better. Guide us to trusted people who can support us and teach us to lean on You when life feels overwhelming. Thank You for offering comfort and rest when we need it most. Amen.

4
THE POWER OF THOUGHTS

___ / ___ / _____

> *"Finally, brothers and sisters, whatever is true, whatever is noble, whatever is right, whatever is pure, whatever is lovely, whatever is admirable—if anything is excellent or praiseworthy—think about such things."*
>
> — PHILIPPIANS 4:8

I've always been a bit of a perfectionist. I want to do my best in everything, whether it's school, sports, or relationships. But sometimes, when things don't go the way I planned, my thoughts take a dark turn. I start telling myself that I'm not good enough or smart enough to succeed. Before I know it, those negative thoughts spiral, leaving me feeling anxious, stressed, and even more stuck.

One day, my youth leader pulled me aside and told me about the power of thoughts. She explained that our thoughts hold a lot of influence over how we feel and behave. When I focus on the negative, it's like I'm feeding my anxiety and stress. But when I focus on what's good, true, and positive, everything feels lighter.

That conversation was a turning point for me. I realized that I had the power to challenge my own thoughts. Whenever something negative crept into my mind—like *"I'm not good enough"*—I replaced it with something true and uplifting. I started telling myself, *"I'm learning and growing"* or *"God has given me strengths I can use."* I also began writing down things I was grateful for every day.

It wasn't always easy, but over time, I noticed a change. My anxiety became more manageable, and I started to feel calmer and more in control. I learned that by focusing on positive thoughts and trusting God, I could take steps toward a healthier mind and heart.

Your Turn

Think about a negative thought you've had recently. Write it down, and then write a positive, truthful thought to replace it. How does focusing on the positive make you feel?

List three things you're grateful for today. How do those blessings remind you of God's care for you?

Prayer

Dear God, thank You for teaching me the power of my thoughts. Help me to replace negativity with truth and to focus on what is good, noble, and pure. I trust You to guide my mind and bring peace when I feel overwhelmed. Thank You for being with me every step of the way. Amen.

5
FAITH, ANXIETY, AND STRESS - OH MY!

___ / ___ / _____

"Do not be anxious about anything, but in every situation, by prayer and petition, with thanksgiving, present your requests to God."

— PHILIPPIANS 4:6

*Y*ou've probably had moments when worry takes over—about schoolwork, relationships, or your future. You might feel like you're carrying it all alone, and it's hard to know what to do. That's exactly how Lily felt.

Lily was overwhelmed by stress until her friend Rachel invited her to a youth group meeting at church. At first, she wasn't sure if it would help, but she decided to go. During the meeting, the speaker shared how faith can make a difference when dealing with anxiety and stress. They read Philippians 4:6 and talked about how prayer and thanksgiving can bring comfort in difficult times.

The next time Lily felt anxiety creeping in, she closed her eyes and prayed. She thanked God for the good things in her life and asked for strength to face her challenges. To her surprise, this small act of faith helped her feel calmer and more grounded.

What about you? When life feels overwhelming, do you pause to give your worries to God? Prayer and faith are powerful tools that can shift your perspective and bring peace. As you lean on God, you'll find that He offers courage, hope, and strength for every moment of stress.

Your Turn

Reflect on a time when you felt anxious or overwhelmed. Did you turn to God in that moment?

How could faith help you handle similar situations in the future?

Make a list of three things you're grateful for today and thank God for them in prayer.

Prayer

Dear God, thank You for being my source of peace when life feels overwhelming. Help me to trust You with my worries and to remember to pray and give thanks in every situation. Teach me to rely on You for strength and wisdom, and help me to see Your goodness in the midst of stress and anxiety. Amen.

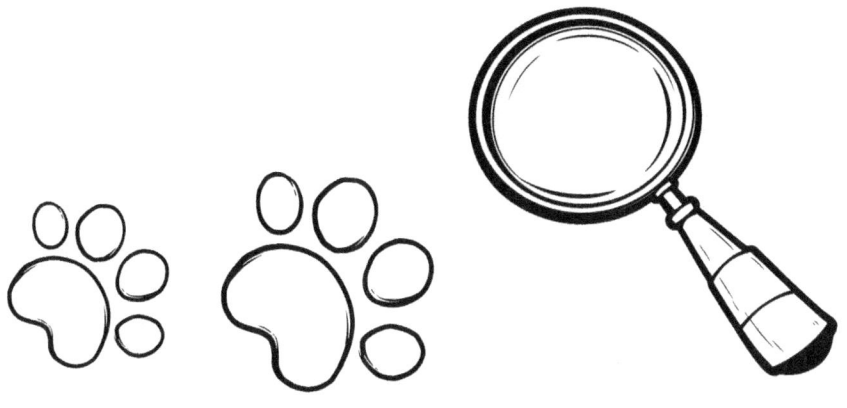

Week 2

Identify Your Triggers

6
TECHNIQUE SPOTLIGHT: BODY SCAN

___ / ___ / _____

Body Scan

The body scan is a mindfulness-based stress reduction technique that involves paying attention to sensations in different parts of the body in a non-judgmental way. This method can help reduce anxiety and stress by bringing your awareness to the present moment and promoting relaxation.

Here's an example of a body scan exercise:

1. Find a quiet and comfortable place where you can sit or lie down without being disturbed for the next 10–15 minutes.
2. Close your eyes and take a few deep breaths to relax your body and mind.
3. Begin to focus your attention on the sensations in your feet. Notice any sensations, such as warmth, tingling, or pressure. Simply observe these sensations without judging them.
4. Move your attention slowly up your body, scanning each body part from your feet to your head. Spend a few seconds on each area, noticing any sensations you feel.

TECHNIQUE SPOTLIGHT: BODY SCAN

5. If you notice any tension or discomfort in a particular area, take a deep breath and direct your attention to that area. Imagine breathing in relaxation and breathing out tension as you focus on that area.
6. Continue to move your attention up your body, noticing any sensations in each body part, until you reach the top of your head.
7. Take a few deep breaths and notice how your body feels now compared to when you started the exercise.

The body scan can be done for any length of time, but starting with shorter sessions of 5–10 minutes can be helpful for beginners. Regular practice of the body scan can help increase your self-awareness and promote relaxation, making it an effective technique for managing stress and anxiety.

What part of your body felt the most relaxed or calm during the body scan? Why do you think that is?

Did you notice any tension or discomfort in your body? How did focusing on it and breathing through it make you feel?

_____

_____

_____

_____

_____

_____

_____

7
SCHOOL

___ / ___ / _____

"Do not let your hearts be troubled. Trust in God; trust also in me."

— JOHN 14:1

*E*mma was feeling nervous about her upcoming presentation. Despite hours of preparation, the thought of standing in front of her classmates and speaking left her feeling anxious and overwhelmed. She noticed how confident some of the other girls in her class seemed, which only made her feel more insecure about her abilities.

As the presentation day approached, Emma's anxiety grew. However, she remembered a verse she had read in the Bible: *"Do not let your hearts be troubled. Trust in God; trust also in me."* This verse gave her a sense of reassurance. She decided to take a deep breath and say a prayer, asking God for strength and guidance.

When the time came, Emma stood in front of the class. Her voice was shaky at first, but she reminded herself to focus on what she had prepared rather than comparing herself to others. As she spoke, her nerves began to subside. By the end of her presentation, Emma felt more confident and was even able to enjoy the experience.

Afterward, Emma received positive feedback from her classmates and teacher. She realized that her own insecurities and fears had been holding her back. With God's help and her own effort, she was able to overcome those doubts and deliver a successful presentation.

Emma's story is a reminder that it's easy to get caught up in comparisons and let insecurities hold us back. But we are all unique creations of God, with our own talents and strengths. By focusing on those strengths and putting trust in God, we can overcome anxiety and accomplish our goals.

Your Turn

Think of a time when you felt nervous or insecure about a school task. What helped you get through it? Write about the experience and how you overcame your fears.

List one or two strategies that can help you feel more confident in stressful situations.

Prayer

Dear God, please help us overcome our insecurities and anxieties, especially in challenging situations like school. Remind us that we are created in Your image, with unique abilities and strengths. Teach us to trust in You and rely on Your wisdom and guidance. Thank You for always walking with us through life's challenges. Amen.

8
RELATIONSHIPS

___ /___ / _____

"Love one another with brotherly affection. Outdo one another in showing honor."

— ROMANS 12:10 (ESV)

I've always considered myself a social person. I love spending time with friends and meeting new people. But when I started high school, something changed. I found myself worrying more about what others thought of me—whether my friends really liked me or whether the new guy in my class noticed me. It started to feel overwhelming, and I didn't know what to do.

One day, my mom shared a verse with me from Romans 12:10: *"Love one another with brotherly affection. Outdo one another in showing honor."* At first, I wasn't sure what it meant, but my mom explained that it's about focusing on treating others with kindness and respect, no matter how they treat you in return.

The more I thought about it, the more I realized something important: I was spending too much time worrying about what people thought of me instead of focusing on how I could show love to others. So, I decided to make a change.

I started doing little things to show my friends I cared—complimenting them, listening more, and being there when they needed me. I even stepped out of my comfort zone and struck up a conversation with the new guy in class, not because I wanted him to like me, but because I wanted to be kind.

To my surprise, the more I focused on showing love and kindness, the less anxious I felt. My relationships became more genuine, and my stress about what others thought of me started to fade away. It reminded me that when I put God's teachings into practice, it not only helps others but brings peace to my own heart as well.

Your Turn

Think of one way you can show kindness or love to someone in your life today. Write about what you'll do and how it could impact your relationship.

Reflect on a time when you worried too much about what others thought. How could focusing on kindness and God's love have made a difference?

Prayer

Dear God, thank You for teaching me the importance of showing love and kindness to others. Help me to focus less on what people think of me and more on how I can honor You through my actions. Remind me that treating others with respect and care is a way to reflect Your love. Thank You for the peace and joy that come from putting You first. Amen.

9
SOCIAL MEDIA

___ / ___ / _____

"Do not conform to the pattern of this world, but be transformed by the renewing of your mind. Then you will be able to test and approve what God's will is—his good, pleasing, and perfect will."

— ROMANS 12:2

Chloe, like many teens, spent hours scrolling through social media. Instagram, TikTok, and Twitter were her go-to apps to stay connected, but over time, they left her feeling anxious and overwhelmed. She couldn't stop comparing herself to others, who seemed prettier, cooler, or happier. Hurtful comments from strangers only made her feel worse, and she started questioning if she was enough.

One day, Chloe saw a post that said, *"Social media is just a highlight reel. Don't compare your behind-the-scenes to someone else's highlight reel."* It hit her hard. She realized she was only seeing the best moments of people's lives, not their struggles.

Chloe decided to take a break from social media and focus on herself. She talked to her parents and friends, who encouraged her to explore hobbies like journaling and painting. Spending time with loved ones helped her feel supported, and the less she compared herself to others, the more confident she became.

Social media can be fun, but it's important to remember it doesn't show the full picture of anyone's life. By focusing on your strengths and surrounding yourself with positivity, you can overcome the stress and anxiety it sometimes brings.

Your Turn

Think about how social media makes you feel. Write about one positive and one negative experience you've had online. How did they affect your mood?

Imagine a social media-free day. What would you do with that time? Write down a few ideas for activities or hobbies you could enjoy.

Prayer

Dear God, thank You for making me fearfully and wonderfully made. Help me focus on my strengths and see myself through Your eyes. Protect me from negativity and guide me toward uplifting people. Give me courage to step away when needed and joy in who You created me to be. In Jesus' name, Amen.

10
HEALTH

___ /___ / _____

"Beloved, I pray that all may go well with you and that you may be in good health, as it goes well with your soul."

— 3 JOHN 1:2

Olivia was always on the go. Between cheerleading, school, and hanging out with her friends, she rarely stopped to take a breath. She loved being part of the team and making memories with her friends, but trying to keep up with everything left her feeling drained.

Olivia also lived with a health condition that required regular medical appointments and treatments. In her effort to keep up with her busy schedule, she sometimes forgot to take care of herself—pushing through exhaustion and skipping meals to make time for her activities. It wasn't long before Olivia began feeling overwhelmed, both physically and emotionally.

One day, Olivia's cheerleading coach shared a devotion based on 3 John 1:2. The coach talked about the importance of balancing a busy life with caring for your body and soul. As Olivia listened, she realized that she had been neglecting her own well-being while trying to stay connected with everyone around her.

Encouraged by the message, Olivia decided to take small but meaningful steps to care for herself. She began setting aside quiet moments to rest, making sure she ate balanced meals, and even learning to say no when she needed time to recharge. At first, it wasn't easy—she worried about disappointing her friends or missing out on fun moments. But as Olivia made these changes, she discovered she had more energy and felt more at peace.

Olivia also leaned on her faith during this journey, trusting that God wanted her to thrive, not just survive. She learned that taking care of herself didn't mean she was letting others down. Instead, it allowed her to be the best version of herself for her friends, her team, and God's plan for her life.

Your Turn

Think about your schedule: Is there something you could adjust to make more time for rest or self-care? Write down one small change you could make and how it might improve your health and mood.

Reflect on a time when you felt overwhelmed trying to do everything. How could you approach a similar situation differently next time?

Prayer

Dear God, thank You for reminding us that our well-being matters to You. Help us to care for our bodies, minds, and souls, even when life feels busy. Teach us to rest in Your presence and find strength in trusting You with our needs. Thank You for walking with us every step of the way. Amen.

11

TECHNIQUE SPOTLIGHT: RELAXATION TECHNIQUES

___ / ___ / _____

Relaxation Techniques

Relaxation techniques are simple and practical ways to help reduce stress and calm your mind. These methods focus on slowing your thoughts, relaxing your body, and grounding yourself in the present moment.

Below are some steps to guide you as you practice relaxation:

1. **Find a Quiet Space:** Choose a calm, distraction-free environment where you can focus for a few minutes.
2. **Get Comfortable:** Sit or lie down in a comfortable position. Close your eyes if it helps you feel more at ease.
3. **Follow the Steps:** Focus on the instructions for the specific relaxation method you're trying, whether it involves breathing, mindfulness, or gentle movements.
4. **Take Your Time:** Allow yourself the freedom to move at your own pace and repeat the process if needed.
5. **Reflect:** After the exercise, spend a moment reflecting on how you feel. Consider noting any changes in your mood or

TECHNIQUE SPOTLIGHT: RELAXATION TECHNIQUES

energy level.

These techniques can be practiced anywhere and adapted to suit your needs. Whether you have a few minutes or a longer period of time, relaxation can help bring peace and balance to your day.

How did you feel before and after practicing the relaxation technique? What differences did you notice in your body or mind?

What relaxation method worked best for you, and how can you include it in your daily routine?

_____

_____

_____

_____

_____

_____

_____

_____

_____

_____

_____

_____

_____

_____

_____

12
DEEP BREATHING

___ /___ / _____

> *"Do not be anxious about anything, but in every situation, by prayer and petition, with thanksgiving, present your requests to God."*
>
> — PHILIPPIANS 4:6

*Y*our days might feel overwhelming sometimes. Between school, activities, and maybe even a part-time job, it's easy to feel like you're always rushing and never catching your breath. That's how Rachel felt—anxious, tense, and unsure of how to slow down. But when a friend suggested deep breathing, she decided to give it a try.

Imagine yourself finding a quiet spot, just like Rachel did. You sit down, close your eyes, and take a deep breath in, counting to four. Hold it for another four seconds, and then slowly exhale for four. You repeat this cycle a few times, focusing on the sensation of your breath moving in and out. As you do, you start to notice something incredible—your shoulders relax, your heartbeat slows, and your mind feels clearer.

DEEP BREATHING

Deep breathing is a simple but powerful way to manage stress. It helps you calm your mind, focus on the present moment, and remind yourself that God is with you, even in your busiest days. By pausing for just a few minutes, you can step away from the chaos and feel His peace.

Your Turn

Find a quiet spot to practice deep breathing for 2–3 minutes. How does it make you feel? Write about your experience and whether you felt calmer or more relaxed afterward.

Think of a time when you felt anxious or overwhelmed. How might deep breathing help you the next time you face a similar situation?

Prayer

Dear God, thank You for the peace that comes from slowing down and focusing on You. Help me to take time during my day to breathe deeply and trust in Your presence. Remind me that I can always turn to You for calm and strength, even when life feels overwhelming. Amen.

13
PROGRESSIVE MUSCLE RELAXATION

___ / ___ / _____

"Be still, and know that I am God."

— PSALM 46:10A

I've always struggled with anxiety and stress, especially during exams. My heart races, my palms get sweaty, and my thoughts start to spiral out of control. I've tried deep breathing exercises before, but they didn't seem to make much of a difference. Then, my counselor introduced me to something called progressive muscle relaxation.

At first, I wasn't sure it would work, but I decided to give it a try. The technique involved tensing and then relaxing different muscle groups in my body. It sounded simple, but as I followed the steps—starting with my toes and working my way up to my head—I could actually feel the tension melting away. When I tried it during my next exam, I was amazed at how calm and focused I felt.

The more I practiced progressive muscle relaxation, the more I realized how helpful it was, not just during exams but in other stressful situations too. Whether I was about to speak in front of a group or meeting new people, this technique helped me feel grounded and present.

Through this practice, I learned the importance of being still and reconnecting with my body. It reminded me that God's peace is always available, and taking a few minutes to intentionally relax can make a big difference in my overall well-being.

Your Turn

Practice progressive muscle relaxation by tensing and relaxing each muscle group in your body, starting with your feet and working your way up to your head. How does this practice affect how you feel? Write about your experience.

Think about a time when you felt stressed or anxious recently. How could using this technique help you handle similar situations in the future?

Prayer

Dear God, thank You for reminding me to be still and know that You are with me. Help me to use tools like progressive muscle relaxation to manage stress and anxiety and to trust in Your peace during overwhelming moments. Thank You for always providing calm in the midst of life's challenges. Amen.

14
VISUALIZATION

___ / ___ / _____

"For as he thinketh in his heart, so is he."

— PROVERBS 23:7A

Samantha had been feeling overwhelmed lately, as if there was never enough time to get everything done. The constant pressure left her anxious, making it hard to focus on her tasks. One day, her mom suggested she try visualization as a relaxation technique.

At first, Samantha was skeptical, but she decided to give it a try. Her mom guided her through a simple exercise where Samantha imagined herself in a peaceful garden. She focused on the vibrant colors, the soothing sounds of birds chirping, and the gentle fragrance of flowers. As she visualized the serene setting, Samantha began to relax. By the end of the exercise, she felt calmer and more centered.

Samantha realized something important that day—she had the power to control her thoughts and feelings. Visualization became a helpful tool for managing her anxiety. Over time, she found that imagining herself in positive and peaceful scenarios not only reduced her stress but also helped her feel more confident and prepared for challenging situations.

Visualization is a powerful tool for managing stress and anxiety. By focusing on positive images and thoughts, we can calm our minds and shift our perspective. Just as Proverbs reminds us, our thoughts shape who we are. When we intentionally choose peace-filled and uplifting thoughts, we can improve both our mental and emotional well-being.

Your Turn

Think about a peaceful place that makes you feel calm. Write about what it looks like, sounds like, and smells like. Imagine yourself there and reflect on how it makes you feel.

Reflect on a stressful situation you've faced recently. How might visualization help you feel calmer and more prepared next time?

Prayer

Dear God, thank You for the power of our thoughts and the peace You bring. Help us to use tools like visualization to calm our minds and focus on Your goodness. Teach us to see the world through positive and peaceful images, trusting in Your strength and guidance. Amen.

15
MINDFULNESS MEDITATION

___ / ___ / _____

"Be still, and know that I am God."

— PSALM 46:10

*Y*our schedule might feel overwhelming sometimes, with school, sports, hobbies, and spending time with friends and family. It can feel like there's never a moment to breathe. When life gets busy, anxiety and stress can creep in, leaving you unsure of how to cope. That's exactly what Michelle experienced before her mom suggested mindfulness meditation.

Imagine yourself finding a quiet spot to sit down, just like Michelle did. You close your eyes, take a deep breath, and focus on the rise and fall of your chest. As thoughts come into your mind, you simply acknowledge them without judgment and let them drift away like clouds in the sky. You stay calm for a few minutes, letting your body relax and your mind grow quiet.

Mindfulness meditation isn't just about calming down—it's about being fully present in the moment. When you take the time to focus on your breathing and let go of distractions, you're also creating space to connect with God. In those still moments, you can feel His presence and be reminded that He is in control, no matter what challenges you're facing. It's a simple practice that can strengthen both your mental well-being and your faith.

Mindfulness meditation can be a powerful way to manage anxiety and stress. By bringing your focus to the present moment, you can calm your racing thoughts and feel God's peace. The Bible reminds you to "be still, and know that I am God." When you take time to pause and focus, you open yourself up to feel His presence more deeply in your life.

Your Turn

Take 5–10 minutes to try mindfulness meditation. If you like, you can try a guided youtube video or an app like Headspace. How did it feel to take a break and center your mind? Write about your experience and whether it helped you feel calmer.

Think about your daily routine. How can you make space for mindfulness meditation? Morning, evening, or in a quiet moment during your day—what time works best for you?

Prayer

Dear God, thank You for reminding me to be still and know that You are always with me. Help me to take time out of my busy day to pause, focus on You, and let go of stress and anxiety. Teach me to trust in Your peace and presence, especially in overwhelming moments. Amen.

Week 4

Develop Healthy Habits

16
TECHNIQUE SPOTLIGHT: GRATITUDE JOURNALING

___ / ___ / _____

Gratitude Journaling

Gratitude journaling is a simple yet effective technique for managing stress and anxiety. It involves regularly writing down things that you are grateful for, which helps shift your focus from negative thoughts to positive ones.

Here's an example of how to practice gratitude journaling:

1. Find a quiet and comfortable place where you can write without distractions.
2. Set a timer for 5–10 minutes. This will help you stay focused and ensure that you don't spend too much time writing.
3. Begin by writing down three things that you are grateful for. They can be big or small, recent or past experiences. For example, "I am grateful for my supportive friends," "I am grateful for the beautiful weather today," "I am grateful for the delicious breakfast I had this morning."
4. Write a sentence or two explaining why you are grateful for each item on your list. This will help you reflect on the

TECHNIQUE SPOTLIGHT: GRATITUDE JOURNALING

positive aspects of your life and deepen your appreciation for them.

For example:

- "My supportive friends always make me feel loved and cared for."
- "The beautiful weather today allowed me to spend more time outside and enjoy nature."
- "The delicious breakfast I had this morning gave me the energy I needed to start my day on a positive note."

Repeat this exercise every day, either in the morning or before bed. Over time, you will begin to notice a shift in your mindset as you become more focused on the positive aspects of your life.

How did writing about the things you're grateful for make you feel today? Did it help shift your mood or perspective?

What's one small thing you might have overlooked before that you're now grateful for? How can you make noticing these moments a habit?

_____

_____

_____

_____

_____

_____

_____

17
EXERCISE AND FITNESS

___ /___ / _____

"Blessed is the one who perseveres under trial because, having stood the test, that person will receive the crown of life that the Lord has promised to those who love him."

— JAMES 1:12

Sometimes life can feel overwhelming and stressful, and you might wonder how to manage everything on your plate. Exercise can be a powerful way to clear your mind and take care of both your body and spirit. Just like Imani, you might hesitate to try something new, but stepping out of your comfort zone could be just what you need.

Imagine joining a dance class or finding an activity that excites you. As you move to the rhythm, focusing on the steps, your worries start to fade. The physical movement energizes your body while the focus on the present moment brings calm to your mind. You might find, just like Imani did, that exercise not only improves your mood but also helps you sleep better and feel more balanced overall.

Taking care of your physical health is just as important as nurturing your spiritual health. God created your body as a gift, and making healthy choices like incorporating exercise into your routine is one way to honor that gift. Whether it's dancing, walking, or any activity you enjoy, even a few minutes of movement each day can make a big difference in how you feel physically and mentally.

Remember, exercise doesn't have to be intense or time-consuming. It's about finding something you love and making it a regular part of your life. When you prioritize movement, you're not just taking care of your body—you're also creating space for God to renew your mind and spirit.

Your Turn

Think about a form of exercise or movement that you enjoy or would like to try. Write about why it excites you and how it could make a difference in your life.

Reflect on your daily routine. Where can you fit in 10 minutes of physical activity to take care of your body and mind?

Prayer

Dear God, thank You for giving me a body that can move and grow stronger. Help me to take care of it by making healthy choices, like finding ways to incorporate exercise into my daily routine. Teach me to honor You by caring for the body You've given me, and guide me toward activities that refresh both my mind and spirit. Amen.

18
HEALTHY EATING & DRINKING

___ / ___ / _____

"Do not be among those who give themselves to wine-drinking, or among those who make themselves full with meat."

— PROVERBS 23:20

*E*mily loved spending time with her friends, watching movies, and trying out new recipes. Recently, she noticed that she had been feeling more anxious than usual and was struggling to sleep well. When she shared this with her mom, her mom suggested that paying attention to what she was eating might help. Healthy eating, she explained, could play a big role in managing stress and anxiety.

Taking her mom's advice, Emily started making small changes to her diet. She included more fruits, vegetables, and lean proteins in her meals and cut back on processed foods and sugary drinks. Instead of soda, she chose water or herbal teas. To her surprise, these adjustments made a noticeable difference. Emily began sleeping better and feeling calmer throughout the day. She realized that the food she put into her body directly impacted how she felt mentally and emotionally.

Our bodies are not just physical vessels; they are temples of the Holy Spirit. When we take care of them through healthy eating and drinking, we glorify God. Emily's experience reminded her of this truth. She learned that making small, intentional changes could not only improve her physical health but also nurture her emotional well-being.

Research shows that good nutrition is closely linked to mental health. A diet rich in fruits, vegetables, whole grains, and lean proteins can help reduce anxiety and stress, while a diet high in processed foods and sugary drinks can worsen those feelings. Building healthy habits, even as a teenager, sets the foundation for a healthier future. Like Emily, anyone can make small changes that lead to significant benefits—one step at a time.

Your Turn

Think about some of your favorite healthy foods or drinks. How can you include them more often in your meals? Write down your ideas.

Reflect on how you feel after eating a balanced meal. How might making small changes to your diet help you manage stress or improve your mood?

Prayer

Dear God, thank You for giving us amazing bodies to take care of. Help us make healthy choices that keep us strong and focused. Teach us to honor You with the way we eat and live every day. Amen.

19

GOOD SLEEP HYGIENE

___ / ___ / _____

"In peace I will lie down and sleep, for you alone, Lord, make me dwell in safety."

— PSALM 4:8

*L*ately, I've been struggling with sleep. Falling asleep has been hard, and even when I do sleep, I find myself waking up in the middle of the night, unable to rest peacefully. The lack of sleep has left me feeling anxious and drained during the day.

One day, I shared my struggles with my friend Suzie, and she suggested that I focus on building better sleep hygiene habits. She explained that sleep hygiene is all about creating healthy routines and practices to improve the quality of sleep. She reminded me that sleep is so important for managing anxiety and stress because it helps regulate our emotions and restore our bodies.

Suzie gave me some helpful tips to try: sticking to a regular bedtime, avoiding caffeine before bed, and drinking chamomile tea in the evening. She also suggested I turn off my screens an hour before bedtime and create a relaxing routine to help me wind down. I decided to give her advice a try, even though it felt like a lot of changes at once.

Within just a few days, I noticed a difference. I was falling asleep faster and staying asleep through the night. I woke up feeling more rested and less anxious. It amazed me how these small changes to my nightly routine could make such a big impact on my mental and emotional health.

Now, I understand how valuable sleep is—not just for my body, but for my overall well-being. Creating a bedtime routine has helped me feel more in control of my stress, and it's become a time to pause and thank God for His peace and protection as I rest.

Your Turn

Write down your current bedtime routine. What small changes can you make to improve your sleep hygiene?

Reflect on how you feel after a good night's sleep. How does it impact your mood and ability to handle stress?

Prayer

Dear God, thank You for the gift of rest and the peace that comes with a good night's sleep. Help me to develop better sleep habits and to make rest a priority in my life. Teach me to trust You and find comfort in Your presence, knowing You will keep me safe and restore my strength as I sleep. Amen.

20
LIMITING SCREEN TIME

___ / ___ / _____

"For everything in the world—the lust of the flesh, the lust of the eyes, and the pride of life—comes not from the Father but from the world."

— 1 JOHN 2:16

You probably enjoy spending time on your phone or computer—whether it's texting friends, scrolling through social media, or binge-watching your favorite shows. But have you ever noticed how too much screen time can make you feel more anxious or stressed? Maybe you've struggled to sleep at night or found it hard to concentrate on your schoolwork.

If that's the case, why not try limiting your screen time? You could start by setting boundaries for yourself, like avoiding your phone or computer before bed or taking breaks during the day to go for a walk or read a book. When you make these small changes, you might be surprised at how much better you feel. By stepping away from screens, you give your mind a chance to relax, helping you sleep better, feel less overwhelmed, and even focus better on your tasks.

LIMITING SCREEN TIME

Taking breaks from technology is an important part of caring for your mental health. It's easy to get caught up in the constant buzz of notifications, social media, and entertainment, but stepping back allows you to recharge and connect with God and yourself. God designed you for moments of stillness and reflection. By being intentional about limiting screen time, you create space to rest, recharge, and draw closer to Him.

So, take a moment to think about your screen habits. What can you do to set healthy boundaries? Whether it's turning off screens an hour before bed or planning technology-free activities, these small changes can make a big difference in how you feel—both mentally and spiritually.

Your Turn

How do you feel when you spend a lot of time on your phone or computer?

What are some activities you can do instead of spending time on screens?

How can limiting screen time help improve your mental health?

Prayer

Dear God, thank you for creating us with the ability to rest and recharge. Help us to set healthy boundaries for ourselves when it comes to technology and to take regular breaks to be still and connect with You. Guide us in managing our anxiety and stress through healthy habits like limiting screen time. Amen.

Week 5

Set Realistic Goals

21

TECHNIQUE SPOTLIGHT: EVALUATING PRIORITIES

___ / ___ / _____

Evaluating Priorities

The 'Evaluating Priorities' technique involves taking a step back and examining what's truly important in your life. By doing so, you can identify what tasks or responsibilities are causing unnecessary stress and adjust your focus accordingly. This technique can be useful in managing stress and anxiety because it helps you prioritize what's most important and eliminate the nonessential tasks that may be overwhelming you.

To use this technique, follow these steps:

1. Make a list of all the tasks and responsibilities you have in your life. This can include work, school, household chores, social events, etc.
2. Assign a priority level to each task or responsibility. Use a numbering system, with "1" being the highest priority and "3" being the lowest.
3. Take a step back and evaluate your priorities. Look at your list and ask yourself if your priorities align with your overall

TECHNIQUE SPOTLIGHT: EVALUATING PRIORITIES

goals and values.
4. Adjust your priorities as necessary. If you find that certain tasks or responsibilities are causing unnecessary stress and are not aligned with your goals and values, consider delegating or eliminating them altogether.
5. Create a new list of prioritized tasks and responsibilities. Use this list as a guide to help you focus on what's truly important and manage your stress and anxiety more effectively.

Here's an example of how you might use the evaluating priorities technique:

List of tasks and responsibilities

- Work (includes meetings, emails, projects, etc.)
- School (includes classes, homework, studying, etc.)
- Household chores (includes cleaning, cooking, laundry, etc.)
- Social events (includes parties, gatherings, etc.)

Priority level

- Work - 1
- School - 1
- Social events - 2
- Household chores - 3

Evaluation

Upon reflection, you realize that social events are taking up too much of your time and causing unnecessary stress. You realize that your priorities are not aligned with your overall goals and values.

Adjustment

You decide to delegate some of your social responsibilities and limit the number of events you attend. You also decide to prioritize self-care activities such as exercise and meditation.

<u>New list</u>

- Work - 1
- School - 1
- Self-care - 2
- Household chores - 2

Using the evaluating priorities technique can help you manage stress and anxiety by focusing on what's truly important in your life and reducing unnecessary tasks and responsibilities.

What tasks or responsibilities are currently taking up most of your time and energy? Do they align with your goals and values?

Are there any tasks or commitments causing you unnecessary stress that you could delegate or let go of?

_____
_____
_____
_____
_____
_____
_____
_____

22
FACING THE FEAR OF FAILURE

___ / ___ / _____

"For God gave us a spirit not of fear but of power and love and self-control."

— 2 TIMOTHY 1:7

Samantha had always been an overachiever. Her goals were ambitious, and she worked tirelessly to reach them. Yet, as her exams approached, an unwelcome sense of fear began to creep in. The idea of failing loomed large in her mind, making her doubt herself. She worried about disappointing her parents, her teachers, and even herself. The more she tried to push these thoughts aside, the heavier they felt, making it harder for her to focus.

One evening, Samantha decided to share her feelings with her friend Olivia. It wasn't easy to admit how overwhelmed she felt, but Olivia listened with understanding. Olivia had dealt with similar fears in the past and shared how she had learned to break her goals into smaller, more manageable steps. She explained that focusing on one step at a time made the bigger picture feel less overwhelming.

Taking Olivia's advice, Samantha sat down and mapped out a study plan. She divided her subjects into smaller sections, set realistic daily goals, and gave herself rewards for completing each one. With each small accomplishment, Samantha felt her confidence grow. Her fear began to shrink, and she realized that failing wasn't the end of the world—it was a part of learning and growing.

Through this process, Samantha discovered that fear doesn't have to control her. With careful planning, support from loved ones, and trust in God, she found the strength to face her challenges. She learned to see setbacks as opportunities to grow, not as reasons to give up. Her journey reminded her that God has equipped her with the tools she needs: a spirit of power, love, and self-control.

Your Turn

Think of a time when you felt afraid of failing. Write about what caused those feelings and how they affected you.

Imagine breaking a big goal into smaller, manageable steps. What would those steps look like? Write them down and describe how it could help reduce your stress or fear.

Prayer

Dear God, thank you for giving us the courage to face our fears and the wisdom to see failure as an opportunity for growth. Help us to trust in You and rely on Your strength to guide us through challenges. Teach us to set realistic goals and take small steps forward with faith and perseverance. May we always remember that You have given us a spirit of power, love, and self-control. Amen.

23

THE IMPORTANCE OF PLANNING

___ / ___ / _____

"Commit your work to the Lord, and your plans will be established."

— PROVERBS 16:3

You've got big dreams and goals, but sometimes, it feels like there's just not enough time to get everything done. Maybe you find yourself procrastinating or feeling overwhelmed by all the tasks on your plate. You're not alone. It's easy to feel stuck when you don't know where to start.

One day, you realize that if you want to achieve your goals, you need a plan. So, you grab a notebook and start by making a list of everything you need to do. Then, you prioritize those tasks, setting deadlines for each one. Instead of tackling everything at once, you break bigger projects into smaller, more manageable steps. Suddenly, things don't seem so overwhelming.

As you follow your plan, you notice something amazing—you're more productive, less stressed, and even have time for the things you enjoy. By committing your plans to God and trusting Him to guide you, you find confidence and peace in knowing you're moving forward with purpose.

Planning isn't just about staying organized; it's a way to honor God with your time and talents. When you take the time to prioritize and commit your work to Him, He'll help you achieve your goals and guide you toward success.

Your Turn

Write about a time when you felt overwhelmed by everything you had to do. How did it affect you, and what could you have done differently?

Make a simple plan for one of your current goals. List the steps you need to take and how you can commit that plan to God.

Prayer

Dear God, thank You for the gift of time and the ability to plan. Help me to commit my work to You and trust in Your guidance as I work toward my goals. Give me the discipline to stay organized, the wisdom to prioritize what matters most, and the courage to follow through. May all I do honor You and bring You glory. Amen.

24
CELEBRATING SMALL WINS

___ / ___ / _____

"Do not despise these small beginnings, for the Lord rejoices to see the work begin."

— ZECHARIAH 4:10

I've set big goals for myself before, like improving in a subject or learning a new skill. At first, I'm excited and ready to dive in, but as I keep working, it can feel like I'm barely making progress. Sometimes, I even wonder if I'll ever get there. That's when I remind myself: big goals don't happen overnight. They're built on small, consistent steps, one at a time.

When I focus on smaller steps, everything feels more doable. For example, instead of cramming an entire chapter into one study session, I'll take on one concept at a time. When I finally understand it, I celebrate—maybe with a favorite snack or a short break to listen to music. That small reward lifts my mood and keeps me motivated. Before I know it, I've finished the chapter, and my confidence has grown.

I've learned to celebrate small wins because they remind me that progress is happening, even if it's slower than I'd hoped. Each step forward is proof that I'm capable and that my hard work matters. It's also a chance to thank God for guiding me and to acknowledge the effort I've put in.

These wins aren't just about big academic goals—they show up in everyday life too. Like when I finally start something I've been avoiding or take a quick walk to clear my head after a long day. Even if I don't finish everything, taking a step forward is worth celebrating. I try to remind myself that progress isn't about huge leaps—it's the small, steady steps that count most.

Your Turn

Think about a goal you're working toward. What's one small step you can take today to get closer to achieving it? Write it down and plan a little way to celebrate when you do it.

What's a small win you've celebrated recently? How did it make you feel? Take a moment to reflect and thank God for helping you along the way.

Prayer

Dear God, thank You for helping us reach our goals, one small step at a time. Remind us to celebrate the progress we make and to be kind to ourselves when things don't happen as quickly as we hope. Help us to stay motivated and trust in Your plan as we work toward the bigger picture. Amen.

25
OVERCOMING PROCRASTINATION

___ /___ / _____

"So let's not get tired of doing what is good. At just the right time we will reap a harvest of blessing if we don't give up."

— GALATIANS 6:9 (NLT)

You have a lot on your plate—school assignments, chores, and that long-term project you've been putting off. But sometimes, you find yourself scrolling through social media or binge-watching your favorite shows instead of getting started. It's not that you don't care, but tackling everything feels so overwhelming that it's easier to avoid it altogether. Sound familiar?

One day, your friend shares a simple strategy that's worked for her. She says, *"Try breaking tasks into smaller steps and setting a deadline for each step. It'll feel less overwhelming. And when you finish each step, reward yourself with something small, like watching a funny video or taking a quick break."*

You decide to give it a try. You sit down, break your big task into smaller, manageable chunks, and set a deadline for the first one.

When you complete that first step, you reward yourself with a favorite song or a snack. It feels good to check something off your list, and suddenly, the next step doesn't feel so hard. Little by little, you make progress, and before you know it, you're finished.

Procrastination can be a major obstacle, but it doesn't have to win. By taking small, intentional steps and celebrating your progress along the way, you can overcome that overwhelming feeling and start achieving your goals. Remember, sometimes just starting is the hardest part. If you tell yourself you'll work for five minutes, you might find yourself so in the flow that you don't want to stop. Those little moments of effort add up to something big.

When you focus on taking action, even if it's just a small step, you're sowing seeds for future success. Keep going, and trust that God will guide you to reap the blessings of perseverance and hard work.

Your Turn

Think about a task you've been avoiding. Write down the first small step you can take to get started. What's a small reward you can give yourself after you complete it?

Reflect on a time when you procrastinated. How did it feel once you finally finished the task? Write about what helped you overcome it.

Prayer

Dear God, help me to overcome procrastination and stay focused on the goals You have placed in my heart. Give me the strength and discipline to take small steps each day, trusting that even little efforts can make a big difference. Thank You for the rewards and blessings that come with perseverance. Amen.

26
TECHNIQUE SPOTLIGHT: HUGGING

___ / ___ / _____

Hugging

Hugging is a simple yet powerful technique that can help reduce stress and anxiety. Hugs have been shown to release oxytocin, a hormone that promotes feelings of love and bonding, and can help reduce levels of the stress hormone cortisol.

To practice hugging as a relaxation technique, follow these steps:

1. Find someone you feel comfortable hugging, such as a friend, family member, or significant other.
2. Approach them and ask if they would be willing to give you a hug.
3. If they agree, open your arms and embrace them.
4. Hold the hug for at least 20 seconds, allowing yourself to fully relax into it.
5. Take slow, deep breaths while hugging, focusing on the feeling of warmth and safety that comes with physical touch.
6. After the hug, take a moment to notice how you feel. You may notice a sense of calm and relaxation, and a reduction in

TECHNIQUE SPOTLIGHT: HUGGING

feelings of stress and anxiety.

If you don't have someone to hug, you can also try hugging a stuffed animal or even hugging yourself. The important thing is to focus on the feeling of physical touch and the release of oxytocin that comes with it.

How did you feel before and after the hug? Did you notice any changes in your mood or stress level?

What does physical touch, like hugging, mean to you, and how can it help you feel more connected to the people in your life?

_____
_____
_____
_____
_____
_____
_____
_____
_____
_____
_____
_____
_____

27
IDENTIFYING SUPPORTIVE PEOPLE

___ / ___ / _____

"Two are better than one because they have a good return for their labor: If either of them falls down, one can help the other up. But pity anyone who falls and has no one to help them up."

— ECCLESIASTES 4:9-10

Jade had always been the kind of person who enjoyed her own company. She loved the comfort of a good book or listening to music, and spending time alone felt like a safe space for her. But when life got challenging and stress started to creep in, Jade began to realize that managing her worries all on her own was becoming too much. It became clear to her that she needed others to lean on, but the thought of opening up to someone felt daunting.

One day, Jade met Clara during her art class. Clara had an infectious positivity about her; she always greeted everyone with a warm smile and genuinely seemed to care about others. At first, Jade hesitated, unsure if she could really trust someone with her thoughts. But

Clara's kind and understanding demeanor gave Jade the confidence to strike up a conversation. As they talked more, Jade began to feel a sense of comfort she hadn't known before. Clara was a great listener, offering words of encouragement without judgment.

Over time, Clara introduced Jade to a group of friends who shared her kindness and empathy. For the first time, Jade experienced what it was like to have a circle of people she could turn to for support. These relationships became a source of strength for her, teaching her that she didn't have to face life's struggles alone.

Through this experience, Jade learned that supportive people don't have to be the loudest in the room or the most outgoing. Sometimes, the best support comes from those who quietly listen and truly care. Having these people in her life made a world of difference, and she also realized the importance of being that person for others when they needed help.

Your Turn

Think about someone in your life who has been there for you during a tough time. What qualities made them supportive?

Write about a time when you felt understood and encouraged by a friend or family member. How did that support impact you?

Prayer

Dear God, thank You for placing people in our lives who lift us up when we are struggling. Help us recognize and cherish these supportive relationships. Guide us to be a source of encouragement for others, just as others have been for us. Amen.

28
COMMUNICATION IN RELATIONSHIPS

___ / ___ / _____

"Therefore encourage one another and build each other up, just as in fact you are doing."

— 1 THESSALONIANS 5:11

*Y*ou've probably had times when life feels overwhelming —when deadlines pile up, and everything seems harder to manage. Maybe, like Eden, you hesitate to share your struggles, worried about burdening those around you. But what if someone noticed and cared enough to ask, *"Are you okay?"*

Imagine this: a friend senses something's wrong and reaches out. At first, you might feel tempted to brush it off, saying, *"I'm fine,"* even though you're not. But what if they gently encouraged you to open up? Sharing your thoughts, even if hesitant at first, could lift a weight off your shoulders. You'd discover that being vulnerable isn't a sign of weakness—it's a step toward healing.

When someone listens to you without judgment, offering words of encouragement and understanding, it strengthens the bond between you. Their support reminds you that you're not alone and that God places people in your life to help carry your burdens.

Good communication is about more than sharing good times; it's trusting others with the hard moments too. When you're open about your struggles, you allow others to support you, and in turn, you can do the same for them. It's through these honest conversations that relationships grow deeper, and you're reminded of God's love working through the people around you.

Your Turn

Who's someone you trust that you could open up to about something weighing on your heart? Take a moment to think about it and plan how you could start that conversation.

Can you recall a time when someone's encouragement helped you through a tough moment? Write about how it felt and what it meant to you.

Prayer

Dear God, thank You for the people who remind us we're not alone. Help us to be honest and vulnerable with those we trust, and give us the courage to listen and encourage others in return. Teach us to speak with love and kindness, building relationships that reflect Your care. Amen.

29
SETTING BOUNDARIES

___ / ___ / _____

"Above all else, guard your heart, for everything you do flows from it."

— PROVERBS 4:23

I used to say *"yes"* to everyone. If someone needed help, I was there. If someone asked me to do something, I'd agree—even when I didn't have the time or energy. I was so afraid of disappointing people or seeming selfish that I constantly put their needs before my own. Eventually, it all caught up to me. I was overwhelmed, stressed, and honestly, a little resentful. That's when I realized I couldn't keep living like this—I needed to make a change.

At first, I didn't even know where to start. I spent some time reflecting on my relationships and noticed that certain people and situations drained me more than others. Slowly, I began to identify what was causing me stress. It was hard to admit, but I knew I needed to set some boundaries. The thought of it made me anxious. Would people think I didn't care? Would they get upset? But I knew I had to prioritize my mental and emotional health.

I started small. I said *"no"* when I couldn't handle something, even though it felt uncomfortable. I carved out time for myself—time to rest, recharge, and take care of the things that mattered to me. I realized that setting boundaries didn't mean shutting people out; it just meant being honest about what I could and couldn't do. To my surprise, most people respected my decisions and even appreciated my honesty. The ones who didn't? I learned they weren't the kind of relationships I needed to hold onto.

Setting boundaries taught me how to love myself better and how to show others how to love and respect me too. It wasn't always easy, but it made a huge difference. I felt more at peace, less overwhelmed, and more confident in how I handled my relationships. Now, I know that protecting my heart isn't selfish—it's an act of self-care and strength.

Your Turn

Who or what tends to drain your energy the most, and why?

What's one thing you could say "no" to this week to take better care of yourself?

Prayer

Dear God, thank You for showing me the importance of guarding my heart and mind. Help me to have the courage to set healthy boundaries and to communicate my needs with kindness and confidence. Teach me how to love myself well so I can love others better. Give me peace as I take steps to protect my well-being and trust You in the process. Amen.

30
BUILDING NEW CONNECTIONS

___ /___ / _____

"Two are better than one, because they have a good return for their labor: If either of them falls down, one can help the other up. But pity anyone who falls and has no one to help them up."

— ECCLESIASTES 4:9-10

*S*tarting somewhere new can be tough. You might miss your old friends or wonder how you'll ever feel like you belong. Maybe you're feeling anxious about meeting new people or putting yourself out there. It's okay—most people feel this way at some point. The good news is, taking that first step to connect with others can lead to some pretty amazing relationships.

Imagine you decide to join a club or activity you're curious about, even if it feels a bit outside of your comfort zone. Maybe it's something like a drama club or a sports team. You might feel nervous at first, but as you get to know the people around you, you start to find things you have in common—shared interests, funny stories, or even goals. It might take time, but you'd likely notice that those small moments of connection can lead to a sense of belonging.

When you take a chance on building new connections, you give yourself the opportunity to grow in ways you never thought possible. Maybe you meet someone who invites you to sit with them at lunch or who shares a passion that inspires you. These small steps can turn into lasting friendships and help you feel more confident and supported.

Building relationships isn't always instant, and it requires effort. You might need to step outside of your comfort zone or take the initiative, but finding common ground with others is a powerful way to feel connected. Over time, you'll discover that the effort is worth it. And remember, God created us for community—you don't have to do it all alone.

Your Turn

Think about a time when you felt alone or isolated. What small step could you take today to meet someone new or connect with someone you already know?

What are some shared interests or activities that you think could help you build relationships with others? Write about one thing you could try this week to reach out.

Prayer

Dear God, thank You for creating us to connect with others. Please give me courage to make new friends, even when it feels hard. Help me find shared interests and trust that these friendships will bring joy and belonging. Amen.

31

TECHNIQUE SPOTLIGHT: A.A.S.P - ANXIETY ATTACK SAFETY PLAN

___ / ___ / _____

A.A.S.P: Anxiety Attack Safety Plan

An 'Anxiety Attack Safety Plan' is a personalized plan developed by individuals who experience anxiety attacks to help them manage their symptoms and minimize the impact of the attack. The plan typically includes strategies to help reduce anxiety and panic symptoms, identify and avoid triggers, and cope with anxiety attacks when they occur.

A typical anxiety attack safety plan may include the following elements:

- **Identify warning signs:** Learn to recognize early warning signs of an anxiety attack. This could include physical sensations such as heart palpitations, shortness of breath, or dizziness.
- **List coping strategies:** Identify coping strategies that work for you. These could include deep breathing exercises, visualization, or other relaxation techniques.

TECHNIQUE SPOTLIGHT: A.A.S.P - ANXIETY ATTACK SAFETY PLAN

- **Develop an action plan:** Develop a specific plan for what you will do when you feel an anxiety attack coming on. This could include moving to a quiet space, practicing relaxation techniques, or seeking support from a friend or family member.
- **Identify support systems:** Identify the people in your life who can offer support during an anxiety attack. This could include a therapist, family member, or friend who understands what you are going through. Know who you can speak to if you need them.
- **Practice self-care:** Make sure to take care of yourself by getting enough sleep, eating a healthy diet, and engaging in physical activity. This can help reduce overall levels of anxiety.

By creating an anxiety attack safety plan, individuals can feel more in control and better equipped to manage their anxiety symptoms when they arise.

What are your early warning signs of an anxiety attack, and how can you recognize them more quickly in the future?

Which coping strategies or support systems do you think will work best for you during an anxiety attack, and why?

_____

_____

_____

_____

_____

Create Your Own A.A.S.P

32

THE POWER OF FACING YOUR FEARS

___ /___ / _____

"Do not be afraid or discouraged, for the Lord will personally go ahead of you. He will be with you; he will neither fail you nor abandon you."

— DEUTERONOMY 31:8

You might find yourself afraid of something that feels impossible to face. Maybe it's public speaking, taking a big test, or even meeting new people. Your heart pounds, your palms sweat, and you wish you could avoid the situation entirely. But what if facing that fear could change your life for the better?

Imagine you're asked to give a presentation in front of your class. At first, the thought feels unbearable. But instead of running from it, you decide to prepare. You practice your speech over and over, learning the material inside and out. As the day arrives, you still feel nervous, but you step up to the podium and begin to speak.

The first few words feel shaky, but as you continue, you realize that fear is starting to fade. By the time you finish, you feel an overwhelming sense of accomplishment. You did it. You faced your fear, and now you know it no longer has control over you.

Facing your fears can be one of the most empowering experiences. It helps you grow in confidence and shows you just how capable you are. When you confront the things that scare you, you grow stronger and more resilient. And as you take on new challenges, you'll see that fear doesn't have to hold you back. With God by your side, you have the strength and courage to overcome anything.

Your Turn

What are some fears you've faced, and how did it feel to overcome them?

What is a current fear you want to overcome?

How can trusting in God help you face challenges with courage?

Prayer

Dear God, thank You for walking with us through our fears. Help us to remember that You are always by our side, giving us the strength to face whatever challenges come our way. Teach us to trust in Your presence and power, and guide us as we grow in courage and resilience. Amen.

33
VISUALIZE SUCCESS

___ /___ / _____

"For as he thinks in his heart, so is he."

— PROVERBS 23:7

Megan was a cheerleader, and the biggest competition of the year was just around the corner. Even though she had practiced with her team for weeks, she couldn't stop feeling nervous about performing in front of the judges and a big crowd. Her mind was filled with self-doubt, and she started questioning if she was good enough. Her coach noticed and introduced her to something called visualization—a way to imagine yourself succeeding to feel more confident and prepared.

At first, Megan wasn't sure it would work, but she decided to try it. At home, she closed her eyes and imagined herself performing the routine perfectly. She pictured every move, heard the cheers of the crowd, and felt the excitement of nailing the routine. The more she practiced this, the more confident she became. She started to believe that she could actually do it.

On the day of the competition, Megan felt nervous again, but instead of letting it take over, she paused, took a deep breath, and remembered the mental image of herself succeeding. When it was time to perform, she focused on each step of the routine, as though she had already done it perfectly in her mind. By the end, the crowd was cheering loudly, and Megan felt a huge sense of accomplishment.

Through visualization, Megan discovered that preparing her mind was just as important as practicing her routine. It helped her overcome her fear and perform with confidence, showing her just how capable she really was.

Your Turn

Think about a time when you felt nervous about something important. How could visualizing yourself succeeding have helped you feel more confident?

Take a moment to reflect on a goal or challenge you're facing right now. What would success look and feel like? Write down the details and imagine yourself achieving it step by step.

Prayer

Dear God, thank You for the gift of visualization and the confidence it can bring. Help us to see ourselves succeeding, even when fear and doubt try to take over. Give us the strength and courage to approach our goals with determination and trust in You. Amen.

34
START SMALL

___ / ___ / _____

"Do not despise these small beginnings, for the Lord rejoices to see the work begin."

— ZECHARIAH 4:10

I've always admired vloggers on social media—their confidence, creativity, and how effortlessly they shared their stories with the world. Deep down, I dreamed of doing the same, but my shyness and fear of being judged held me back. The idea of talking to a camera and putting myself out there seemed overwhelming, so I never tried.

One day, I decided to challenge myself and take a small step toward my dream. I set up a camera in my room and started recording short videos about my daily life. At first, I stumbled over my words and felt awkward, but I reminded myself of the verse, *"Do not despise these small beginnings."* That gave me the courage to keep going.

With each video I recorded, my confidence grew. I experimented with new topics, learned to edit my footage, and started sharing my videos with a few close friends. Their encouragement and kind feedback meant so much to me. I realized that even though I wasn't perfect, I was learning and improving with every step.

As I continued to embrace my passion for vlogging, my fear began to fade. I found so much joy in sharing my authentic self with others. The more vulnerable and real I allowed myself to be, the more fulfillment I experienced. It wasn't just about making videos—it was about stepping out in faith and trusting God with the dreams He placed on my heart.

Starting small has taught me that God celebrates our efforts, no matter how humble they may seem. When we take the first step, He meets us where we are and helps us grow into the person He's called us to be.

Your Turn

What dream or passion do you feel God has placed on your heart?

What small step could you take this week to begin pursuing it?

How might sharing your authentic self with others lead to personal growth and joy?

Prayer

Dear God, thank You for the dreams You've placed in my heart and for celebrating even my smallest steps forward. Help me to trust You as I pursue my passions and to rely on Your strength when I feel unsure. Give me the courage to be vulnerable, to embrace my gifts, and to use them to make a difference in the lives of others. Amen.

35
CELEBRATING PROGRESS

___ / ___ / _____

"The LORD your God is with you, the Mighty Warrior who saves. He will take great delight in you; in his love, he will no longer rebuke you, but will rejoice over you with singing."

— ZEPHANIAH 3:17

You might set high standards for yourself, always striving to excel—whether it's in school, sports, or hobbies. But when you're always pushing forward, it's easy to forget how far you've already come. Have you ever stopped to celebrate the progress you've made?

Imagine if you paused to recognize each step toward your goals. Instead of stressing about what's left to do, you'd take pride in what you've already accomplished. Maybe you've tackled a tough project, learned something new, or overcome a personal challenge. Those small wins matter, and celebrating them can motivate you to keep going.

Progress isn't just about big achievements—it's about the journey and the growth along the way. Every step, no matter how small, brings you closer to your goals. Whether it's learning a new skill, finishing part of a creative project, or simply taking a step outside your comfort zone, each moment is worth recognizing. Take time today to reflect on how far you've come—you deserve to celebrate that!

Your Turn

What small wins have you experienced recently? Write about a time you overcame a challenge or made progress, even if it felt small at the time.

Think about a goal you're currently working on. How can you celebrate the steps you've taken so far to get closer to achieving it?

Prayer

Dear God, thank You for guiding me and for every step of progress I've made. Help me to celebrate small victories and find joy in the process of growth. Teach me to appreciate how far I've come while trusting You to lead me forward. Amen.

Week 8

Develop Coping Strategies

36
TECHNIQUE SPOTLIGHT: BRAIN DUMP

___ / ___ / _____

Brain Dump

The brain dump technique is a helpful way to manage stress and anxiety by clearing your mind of racing thoughts and worries.

Here are some instructions for the exercise:

1. Find a quiet and comfortable place to sit down with a pen and paper or your electronic device.
2. Set a timer for 10-15 minutes.
3. Start writing down every thought that comes to mind, without stopping to think about it or worrying about grammar or punctuation.
4. Write down anything that's on your mind, whether it's a to-do list, worries, or anything else that's causing stress or anxiety.
5. Keep writing until the timer goes off.
6. Once you're done, take a deep breath and review what you've written.

TECHNIQUE SPOTLIGHT: BRAIN DUMP

7. Highlight any important tasks or concerns that you need to address.
8. Write down any potential solutions to these concerns or ways you can take action on the important tasks.
9. Make a plan to address these tasks or concerns, and let go of the other thoughts and worries that are not helpful or productive.

By doing a brain dump exercise regularly, you can clear your mind of unnecessary stress and anxiety and focus on the tasks and concerns that are most important to you.

How did it feel to let go of all your thoughts and write them down? Did it help you feel calmer or more focused?

Looking at what you've written, what's one small step you can take today to address an important task or worry?

_____

_____

_____

_____

_____

_____

_____

_____

_____

37
COPING THROUGH VISUAL ART

___ /___ / _____

> *"He has filled them with skill to do all kinds of work as engravers, designers, embroiderers in blue, purple, and scarlet yarn and fine linen, and weavers—all of them skilled workers and designers."*
>
> — EXODUS 35:35

Thea, a 16-year-old girl, often felt the weight of the world pressing down on her shoulders. The demands of school, relationships, and life in general left her overwhelmed. Yet, amidst the chaos, one thing brought her peace: her love for creating art.

She had always been drawn to various forms of artistic expression—engraving, embroidery, design, and weaving. Whenever Thea felt anxious, she turned to these creative pursuits as a way to express herself and find relief from stress. The rhythmic motion of her hands crafting intricate designs allowed her to focus her mind and feel grounded in the present moment.

As Thea poured herself into her art, she discovered a way to channel her emotions into something tangible and meaningful. Whether it was engraving delicate patterns, weaving colorful textiles, or sketching captivating visuals, each creation became a reflection of her inner world. Her hands brought beauty to life, reminding her of the unique skills and talents God had given her.

Through her creative endeavors, Thea experienced more than just joy and fulfillment. Art became a sanctuary where she found peace, healing, and even connection with God. Each finished piece stood as a testament to her resilience and her ability to find beauty even in challenging times.

Thea's story is a powerful reminder of how art can help us cope with life's struggles. Creative pursuits allow us to express ourselves authentically, find moments of calm, and reflect on the gifts God has given us. When we embrace these talents, we not only grow personally but also find a deeper connection to Him.

Your Turn

Think of a time when you felt stressed or overwhelmed. What creative activity could you try to help ease your mind?

Imagine you are designing something meaningful that reflects your personality or emotions. What would it look like, and why?

Prayer

Dear God, thank You for the unique talents and abilities You have given us. Help us to use these gifts to bring beauty, peace, and healing to ourselves and others. Guide us to find comfort and joy in creative pursuits, and may we use our skills to glorify You and bring light into the world. Amen.

38
THE THERAPEUTIC POWER OF WRITING

___ / ___ / _____

"Cast all your anxiety on him because he cares for you."

— 1 PETER 5:7

I was feeling completely overwhelmed. Anxiety and stress seemed to follow me everywhere, and no matter what coping strategies I tried, nothing really brought lasting relief. Then one day, I decided to try something different—writing. I wasn't sure where it would lead, but I opened a journal and started with small entries about my thoughts and emotions.

As I wrote more, I discovered something powerful. Writing became my outlet, a way to pour out my fears and anxieties onto paper. It was like a weight lifted off my shoulders each time I expressed what I was feeling in words. Journaling helped me organize my thoughts and make sense of my emotions, and I began to feel a sense of clarity that I hadn't experienced in a long time.

Over time, I noticed patterns in my journal entries—triggers, recurring thoughts, and areas that needed my attention. Writing gave me a way to reflect and understand myself better. I felt like I had more control over my emotions, and the act of putting pen to paper became a healing practice for me.

Through writing, I've learned that it can be so much more than just words on a page. It's a way to process challenges, release pent-up feelings, and find peace. Whether it's journaling or storytelling, writing has become a tool for self-awareness and growth. It reminds me that I can navigate life's uncertainties with clarity and strength.

Your Turn

Reflect on a time when you felt overwhelmed. How might writing have helped you process your thoughts and feelings?

Create a list of emotions you've felt recently and write about one of them. How does exploring it through writing make you feel?

Prayer

Dear God, thank You for the gift of writing and the comfort it brings to my heart. Help me to use this gift to process my emotions and lay my anxieties at Your feet. Guide me to see writing as a way to connect with You, find clarity, and heal from the inside out. May my words bring me peace, and may I grow closer to You through this practice. Amen.

39
LISTENING TO MUSIC AS A CALMING TOOL

___ / ___ / _____

"Make a joyful noise to the Lord, all the earth; break forth into joyous song and sing praises!"

— PSALM 98:4

One day, a friend suggests that you try listening to music as a way to calm down and relax. It seems simple, but you decide to give it a shot. You create a playlist of your favorite calming songs and press play.

As you listen, you notice a shift within yourself. The music helps you feel more at ease, your thoughts start to clear, and you find it easier to focus on your tasks. You may even use the music as part of your bedtime routine, helping you wind down and create a peaceful atmosphere in your room. Over time, your playlist becomes an essential part of your self-care routine, helping you manage your stress and anxiety in a healthy way.

The power of music is undeniable. It can shift your mood, slow your breathing, and bring a sense of calm to a chaotic day. Whether you listen to your favorite soothing songs or create a playlist tailored to help you relax, music has the ability to ground and center you. It provides comfort and reminds you that you are not alone.

Sometimes, life feels overwhelming, but tools like music can help. By incorporating calming music into your daily routine, you can create moments of peace and joy, no matter what challenges you face.

Your Turn

Have you ever used music as a way to calm down or relax? How did it make you feel?

What are some of your favorite songs or artists that help you unwind and de-stress?

Prayer

Dear God, thank you for the gift of music. Help us to use it as a tool to manage our anxiety and stress in healthy ways. Guide us as we create playlists and listen to our favorite songs, and help us feel more grounded and centered as we do so. Amen.

40

TIME MANAGEMENT

___ / ___ / _____

"So teach us to number our days, that we may gain a heart of wisdom."

— PSALM 90:12

You've probably experienced the rush to finish assignments, the stress of missing deadlines, and the frustration of feeling like there's no time to relax. When anxiety starts piling up and you don't know what to do, it can feel overwhelming. One day, you decide to seek advice from a friend who seems to have it all together. They share something valuable with you —time management can be a game-changer.

Your friend talks about how creating a schedule, setting priorities, breaking down tasks, and taking regular breaks can help you feel more in control of your time. You take their advice to heart and give it a try. You start by listing all your tasks for the week—homework, studying, work, and extracurricular activities. Next, you prioritize what's most important and schedule time for breaks and relaxation.

As you follow your new schedule, you notice a change. You're able to focus better on your work, reduce procrastination, and still have time for yourself. By managing your time wisely, you find a sense of balance and feel less overwhelmed. Each day becomes an opportunity to be productive without sacrificing your peace of mind.

Time management isn't just about getting things done—it's about learning to live intentionally. When you use your time well, you reduce stress and discover that you're capable of achieving your goals without feeling drained. So, how will you choose to manage your time today?

Your Turn

Think about your current schedule. What are some small changes you could make to manage your time more effectively?

Write down a simple weekly schedule, including your tasks and break times. How would following this plan help reduce stress in your life?

Prayer

Dear God, thank You for the time You've given us. Teach us to manage it wisely so that we can reduce stress and achieve our goals. Help us to prioritize what matters most, stay disciplined, and find balance in our lives. Guide us to use our time in ways that honor You. Amen.

41
TECHNIQUE SPOTLIGHT: PRAYER

___ /___ / _____

Prayer

*P*raying can be an effective way to manage stress and anxiety as it allows individuals to connect with a higher power, express their concerns, and seek guidance and support.

Here's a detailed exercise example for someone to follow along with:

1. Find a quiet and comfortable place to sit or kneel where you won't be disturbed.
2. Take a few deep breaths and focus on the present moment.
3. Start with an opening prayer or a simple greeting, such as *"Dear God"* or *"Heavenly Father."*
4. Express your gratitude for the things you have in your life, such as your family, friends, health, or a roof over your head.
5. Share your worries and concerns, and ask for guidance and strength to overcome them. You can be as specific or general as you like and share as much or as little as you feel comfortable.

TECHNIQUE SPOTLIGHT: PRAYER

6. End your prayer with a closing, such as *"Amen," "In Jesus' name,"* or *"Thank you for listening."*
7. Take a few more deep breaths and sit quietly for a few minutes, reflecting on your prayer and allowing yourself to feel more at peace.

You can repeat this exercise daily or as often as you like and customize it to your personal beliefs and preferences. Some people find it helpful to write down their prayers in a journal or to pray with others, while others prefer to pray silently or out loud. The key is to find what works for you and make it a regular part of your routine.

How do you feel after taking time to pray and share your worries? Did it help bring you a sense of peace or comfort?

What's one thing you're grateful for today that you can include in your prayers moving forward?

_____

_____

_____

_____

_____

_____

_____

_____

_____

42
THE POWER OF PRAYER

___ /___ / _____

Do not be anxious about anything, but in every situation, by prayer and petition, with thanksgiving, present your requests to God. And the peace of God, which transcends all understanding, will guard your hearts and your minds in Christ Jesus."

— PHILIPPIANS 4:6-7

You might feel overwhelmed with schoolwork, personal challenges, or life in general. When nothing seems to ease the stress, have you considered turning to prayer? Prayer isn't just for church—it's a powerful way to manage stress and connect with God.

Take a few minutes each day to pray. Find a quiet spot, thank God for the good things in your life, and share your worries with Him. At first, it might feel like nothing's changing, but over time, you'll notice how much calmer and clearer you feel. Prayer helps you release your burdens and trust that God is at work in your life.

Making prayer a daily habit, whether in the morning or before bed, can bring comfort and strength. Those moments with God help you face life's challenges with a more peaceful heart. And when you share how prayer has helped you with friends or family, you might inspire them to try it too.

Prayer has the power to transform stress into peace and fear into strength. By trusting God and speaking with Him regularly, you can approach life's challenges with renewed hope and confidence.

Your Turn

Think about a time when you felt stressed or anxious. How could prayer help you in those moments?

What are some things you'd like to include in your prayers—whether it's gratitude, requests for guidance, or sharing your worries?

Prayer

Dear God, thank You for the gift of prayer and for always listening when we call on You. Help us turn to You in moments of stress and anxiety, trusting that You will give us peace and strength. Guide us to make prayer a daily habit and remind us that we are never alone because You are always with us. Amen.

43
FINDING COMFORT IN SCRIPTURE

___ /___ / _____

"Your word is a lamp to my feet and a light to my path."

— PSALM 119:105

Poppy had been feeling anxious and stressed lately. Sleep escaped her at night, and her thoughts were filled with worries she couldn't control. She tried everything she could think of to feel better, but nothing seemed to work. Then, one day, her aunt gently suggested something new—turning to scripture for comfort and peace.

Initially, Poppy wasn't sure where to start, but her aunt encouraged her to begin with a passage that held timeless meaning. She opened her Bible to Psalm 23 and began to read. As the words, "The Lord is my shepherd, I shall not want," filled the room, a wave of calm washed over her. For the first time in a while, she felt a sense of reassurance and peace.

Poppy soon made it a daily practice to read scripture before starting her day. Over the following days, she discovered how comforting specific verses could be during anxious moments. Philippians 4:6–7 reminded her not to be anxious but to pray and give thanks. Isaiah 41:10 assured her of God's presence, strength, and help in challenging times. These scriptures became like a soothing balm to her troubled heart.

Through this journey, Poppy learned the importance of finding comfort in scripture. As she read and meditated on God's word, she began to experience peace that carried her through her days. The Bible wasn't just a book anymore—it became her guide, her source of strength, and a reminder that she was never alone, no matter what she faced.

Your Turn

What scripture passages have brought you comfort during challenging times?

How can making time for reading the Bible help you feel more grounded and at peace?

Prayer

Dear God, thank You for the gift of Your word, which brings light to our darkest moments. Help us to remember the comfort and guidance You offer through scripture. Teach us to turn to Your promises in times of anxiety and stress, trusting that You are always with us. Fill our hearts with peace and strength as we draw closer to You. Amen.

44
COMMUNITY AND FELLOWSHIP

___ / ___ / _____

"Let us consider how we may spur one another on toward love and good deeds, not giving up meeting together, as some are in the habit of doing, but encouraging one another—and all the more as you see the Day approaching."

— HEBREWS 10:24-25

I remember a time when I felt so alone and stressed. Everything in my life seemed to pile up all at once, and I didn't know how to handle it. I tried to deal with my problems on my own, but it just made me feel more isolated. One day, a friend invited me to a youth group meeting at their church. I wasn't sure about it at first, but something inside me nudged me to give it a try.

When I arrived, I was surrounded by other teenagers who were going through similar struggles. They shared their stories, offered support, and encouraged one another. For the first time in a long time, I felt like I belonged. I realized I didn't have to face my problems on my own. The warmth of the group and the sense of community gave me a peace I hadn't felt before.

The discussions at the youth group often included faith and how it connects to the challenges we face. It wasn't just about sharing struggles; it was also about reminding one another of God's love and support. Through these meetings, my relationship with God deepened, and I found strength and comfort I hadn't experienced before. I left each meeting feeling encouraged and hopeful.

Being part of a community taught me the importance of fellowship in my faith journey. It reminded me that surrounding myself with supportive people who share my beliefs is essential for managing stress and growing spiritually. Community and fellowship are more than just gatherings; they're spaces where we can find accountability, encouragement, and the reminder that we are never truly alone.

Your Turn

Have you ever felt like you were carrying your struggles all by yourself? Write about how it made you feel.

Think about a time when being with others helped you feel less alone. What did you learn from that experience?

Prayer

Dear God, thank you for the gift of community and fellowship. I'm grateful for the people you've placed in my life to encourage and strengthen my faith. Help me to value these relationships and to be a source of comfort and support for others. May I always find joy in sharing my journey with those who uplift me. In Jesus' name, Amen.

45
HOPE & TRUST IN GOD

___ / ___ / _____

"Trust in the Lord with all your heart and lean not on your own understanding; in all your ways submit to him, and he will make your paths straight."

— PROVERBS 3:5-6

You've been feeling overwhelmed lately—school, relationships, and life's pressures seem to pile on top of each other. Your anxiety feels like it's through the roof, and you find yourself constantly worrying about what's ahead. One day, while scrolling through social media, you stumble upon a post that reads, *"When you feel like you are drowning in life's problems, try to find the strength to trust God and hold on to hope."*

That message strikes a chord. You realize that in the midst of your worries, you've forgotten to trust God. You decide to make a change, to focus on prayer and God's word. You start by reading Proverbs 3:5-6, reflecting on its powerful reminder to surrender your worries and trust in God's plan. Slowly, as you pray and turn your thoughts toward Him, you begin to feel a peace you haven't felt in a long time.

When you put your hope and trust in God, you're reminded that you don't have to carry your burdens alone. Trusting Him doesn't mean you'll never face challenges, but it means that you're not facing them without help. You start to see how relying on God's wisdom and guidance gives you the strength to tackle obstacles with renewed courage. His plan for you is greater than anything you could imagine, and by leaning on Him, you can embrace each step forward with faith.

Through this, you learn that trusting God is an active choice—a daily decision to release control and believe in His goodness. Even when it's hard to understand what's happening around you, you can have faith that He is working all things together for your good. Trusting in God doesn't eliminate the storms, but it helps you find peace in the midst of them.

Your Turn

What's one thing in your life right now that feels overwhelming? How could you trust God with it?

If you could ask God for help with one specific worry, what would it be?

What's one Bible verse or quote that inspires you to have hope? How can you use it to encourage yourself today?

Prayer

Dear God, thank You for being our source of hope and strength. Help us to trust in Your plan, even when life feels overwhelming. Teach us to lean on You and to hold on to hope in difficult times. Guide us in finding peace and assurance through Your word. Amen.

46
TECHNIQUE: PRACTICING SELF-CARE

___ / ___ / _____

Practicing Self-Care

Practicing self-care is an important technique for managing stress and anxiety. Self-care involves taking care of oneself physically, mentally, and emotionally.

Here's a plan for practicing self-care:

1. **Schedule self-care time:** Set aside specific times in your day or week for self-care activities. This could be anything from taking a bubble bath to going for a walk in nature.
2. **Identify self-care activities:** Make a list of activities that you enjoy and that help you feel relaxed and recharged. Some examples include reading a book, listening to music, practicing yoga, or spending time with loved ones.
3. **Prioritize self-care:** Make self-care a priority by incorporating it into your daily routine. This could be as simple as taking a 10-minute break during your workday to practice deep breathing or taking a walk around your neighborhood.

TECHNIQUE: PRACTICING SELF-CARE

4. **Be present in the moment:** When practicing self-care, focus on being present in the moment and fully engaging in the activity. This can help you feel more relaxed and reduce feelings of stress and anxiety.
5. **Adjust your self-care routine:** Pay attention to how your self-care routine is affecting your overall well-being. If certain activities are not helping you feel better, try adjusting your routine and trying new activities.

Remember, practicing self-care is a personal journey and what works for one person may not work for another. It's important to find self-care activities that work for you and that help you feel relaxed and recharged.

What self-care activities help you feel the most relaxed and recharged? How can you make time for them in your routine? Are there any new ones you'd like to try?

How do you feel after practicing self-care? Write about any changes you've noticed in your mood or energy.

_____

_____

_____

_____

_____

_____

_____

_____

47
UNPLUG AND DISCONNECT

___ /___ / _____

"Be still, and know that I am God."

— PSALM 46:10

You might find yourself constantly scrolling through your phone, checking for updates, and staying connected with friends through social media. It feels like the world is right there in your hands, and yet, the more you scroll, the more anxious or restless you feel. Perhaps, like many others, you've noticed the stress building as you struggle to relax. One day, you decide to take a step back—to unplug and disconnect.

At first, you may feel a bit uneasy without your phone. Maybe your fingers itch to check notifications or scroll through your favorite app. But as the hours go by, you start to notice something else: the quiet. You begin to embrace the peace, spending time reading, journaling, or simply enjoying a walk outside. The sound of birds chirping or the warmth of the sun on your face might remind you of how beautiful the simple things in life can be.

Through this time of unplugging, you begin to realize just how much you've been relying on technology to fill the quiet moments. You see how important it is to pause and find joy in being present in the moment. You discover that disconnecting doesn't mean losing out—it means gaining peace and stillness.

Unplugging from technology gives you the chance to focus on what truly matters—your relationship with God, your well-being, and the world around you. When you allow yourself this space, you open the door to enjoy life in its fullness. You might find more joy in conversations, more clarity in your thoughts, and more appreciation for the beauty surrounding you.

Your Turn

Do you ever feel overwhelmed or stressed because of your phone or social media? Write about how it makes you feel.

What are three things you could do to unplug and enjoy some time without technology? Reflect on how those activities could bring you peace.

Think about the last time you truly felt present in the moment. What were you doing, and how did it make you feel?

Prayer

Dear God, help me find peace and stillness in my life. Teach me to unplug and disconnect from technology when I need to focus on the simple joys You've placed around me. Thank You for the moments of calm that refresh my soul and help me draw closer to You. Amen.

48
ENGAGE IN HOBBIES & CREATIVE ACTIVITIES

> *"Each of you should use whatever gift you have received to serve others, as faithful stewards of God's grace in its various forms."*
>
> —1 PETER 4:10

Sophie had always loved drawing and painting. Whenever she felt stressed or anxious, she would pick up her sketchbook and let her creativity flow. However, with school and other responsibilities piling up, Sophie had begun to neglect her passion for art. One day, she realized how much she missed it and decided to set aside some time each week to paint and draw.

As Sophie started painting again, a sense of peace and joy washed over her. She recognized that engaging in her hobby was not only a way to relax but also a way to connect with God. With every brushstroke, she felt His presence, inspiring her to create something beautiful.

Over time, Sophie began to see her artistic talent as a gift from God. She felt a deep sense of purpose in using her talent to bring joy and beauty to others. She started sharing her artwork with friends and family and even volunteered at a local art center to teach children how to paint and draw.

Through her creative pursuits, Sophie discovered a deeper connection with God and a meaningful way to serve others. Her hobby became more than just a pastime—it became a way to glorify God and make a positive impact on the world.

Pursuing hobbies and creative activities is not just about unwinding—it's about honoring the gifts God has given us. By engaging in activities we love, we create opportunities to connect with Him and share His love with others. God has blessed each of us with unique talents and abilities. It's our responsibility to nurture those gifts, allowing them to bring joy, beauty, and hope to those around us.

Your Turn

What's a hobby or creative activity that makes you feel most alive and joyful?

How can you set aside time each week to enjoy that hobby and reconnect with God?

How might your unique talents bring joy to others and reflect God's love?

Prayer

Dear God, thank you for the unique talents and abilities you have given each of us. Help us to use them to serve others and glorify You. Guide us as we pursue our hobbies and creative activities, and help us find joy and fulfillment in them. Amen.

49
HAVE A MENTAL HEALTH DAY

___ / ___ / _____

"Come to me, all you who are weary and burdened, and I will give you rest."

— MATTHEW 11:28

I had been feeling completely overwhelmed. Between school, extracurricular activities, and keeping up with my social life, it felt like I never had a moment to breathe. My anxiety was getting worse, and I knew I needed to do something to take care of myself. One day, I decided to take a mental health day.

I stayed home and spent the day doing things that brought me joy. I took a long bath, listened to my favorite music, and read a book I'd been wanting to finish. Later, I went for a walk in the park and sat by the lake, simply enjoying the peaceful surroundings. It was a day just for me, and I finally felt like I could breathe again.

As I sat there by the water, I thought about how important it is to take care of my mental health. Life gets so busy that I sometimes forget to prioritize my own well-being. But as I rested, I realized that taking time to relax and recharge isn't selfish—it's necessary. When I take the time to do the things that make me happy and help me relax, I come back to my responsibilities feeling refreshed and ready.

I reflected on Matthew 11:28, where Jesus invites those of us who are weary and burdened to come to Him for rest. It reminded me that I don't have to carry everything on my own. Taking care of myself not only helps me feel better but also makes space for me to connect with God and allow Him to restore my heart and mind.

Your Turn

What's one thing you've done recently just for yourself, and how did it make you feel?

If you could design your perfect mental health day, what would it include?

Why do you think it's important to take breaks when life gets overwhelming?

Prayer

Dear God, thank you for always being there for me when I feel weary and burdened. Help me to remember to take care of myself and prioritize my mental health, so I can be my best self for You and for others. Thank You for giving me rest and peace when I come to You. Amen.

50
SAY NO TO THINGS THAT DRAIN YOU

___ / ___ / _____

"Let your 'Yes' be 'Yes,' and your 'No,' 'No.' For whatever is more than these is from the evil one."

— MATTHEW 5:37

You may find yourself constantly saying yes to others, always wanting to help and make everyone happy. Maybe you volunteer for every activity or event, even when your schedule is already overflowing. But have you ever stopped to think about how all of this might be affecting you? When you take on too much, it can leave you feeling overwhelmed and stressed.

One day, a friend might ask you to help with something big—like planning a surprise party. You want to help because you care, but deep down, you know it will stretch you too thin. Saying no isn't easy, but it's necessary. Taking a deep breath, you politely explain why you can't help this time. You realize it's okay to prioritize your well-being.

At first, you might feel a little guilty for saying no. But as you see others find alternative solutions, you begin to understand that it's not selfish to set boundaries. In fact, saying no can protect your mental health and energy. It allows you to focus on what truly matters and ensures you have time to rest and recharge.

Setting boundaries doesn't mean you're being rude or uncaring. It means you value your health and well-being enough to make wise decisions. When you say no to things that drain you, you open the door to a healthier, more balanced life.

Your Turn

Think about a time when you felt overwhelmed because you couldn't say no. What happened, and how did it make you feel?

What are some ways you can practice saying no kindly but confidently?

How can setting boundaries help you feel more at peace in your day-to-day life?

Prayer

Dear God, help me to recognize when I need to say no and set boundaries to protect my time and well-being. Remind me that it's okay to prioritize my needs and guide me in communicating with kindness and love. Give me the strength to make choices that lead to peace and balance. Amen.

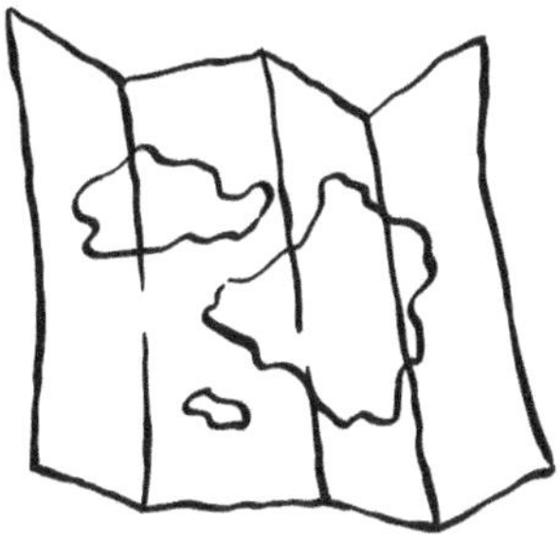

51
TECHNIQUE SPOTLIGHT: EMBRACE WHAT RESONATES

___ / ___ / _____

Embrace What Resonates

As we reach the final week of our journey together, it's time to reflect on the techniques and strategies we've explored throughout the book. Each week, we discussed various approaches to managing stress and anxiety, empowering you to find what works best for you. This week, your task is to embrace what resonates with you and make it a cornerstone of your personal well-being practice.

Here's how you can approach this technique:

1. **Reflect on the weeks prior:** Take a moment to reflect on the different techniques and strategies we've discussed in the previous weeks. Which ones stood out to you? Which ones resonated with your experiences and preferences? Recall the moments when you felt a sense of connection or inspiration as we explored different practices.
2. **Choose your favorites:** Select a few techniques that truly spoke to you. These could be mindfulness exercises, relaxation techniques, coping strategies, self-care practices,

TECHNIQUE SPOTLIGHT: EMBRACE WHAT RESONATES

or any other approaches that deeply resonated with your needs and values. Consider the ones that you found most effective or enjoyable during our journey.

3. **Personalize and integrate:** Take the techniques you've chosen and personalize them to fit your unique circumstances and preferences. Adapt them to align with your schedule, lifestyle, and personality. Make them your own by adding any modifications or creative touches that enhance your experience.
4. **Create a routine:** Establish a regular practice incorporating your chosen techniques. Designate specific times during your day or week to engage in these practices. Consistency is key to deriving the most benefit from them. By incorporating them into your routine, you are prioritizing your well-being and creating space for growth and healing.
5. **Reflect and adjust:** As you engage in these techniques, reflect on how they impact your well-being. Notice any changes in your stress levels, anxiety symptoms, and overall sense of calm. Be open to adjustments and modifications along the way. What works best for you may evolve over time, so stay attuned to your needs and make necessary adaptations.
6. **Share and inspire:** If you find certain techniques particularly beneficial, don't hesitate to share them with others. Discuss your experiences with friends, family, or a support group. By sharing what has worked for you, you may inspire others on their own journeys of self-discovery and well-being.

Remember, the goal of this technique is to embrace what resonates with you and create a sustainable practice that supports your ongoing well-being. By choosing techniques that align with your values and preferences, you are empowering yourself to take charge of your mental and emotional health.

BIBLICAL TEACHINGS

Which technique or strategy from this book has resonated with you the most? How has it made a difference in your life?

How will you incorporate your favorite technique into your daily or weekly routine? Write down specific steps to make it a regular part of your life.

52
REFLECTING ON PROGRESS

___ / ___ / _____

"Give thanks in all circumstances; for this is God's will for you in Christ Jesus."

— 1 THESSALONIANS 5:18

You sit on your bed, flipping through the pages of your journal. For the past three months, you've been jotting down your thoughts and feelings as you work to manage your anxiety and stress. As you read, you notice how much progress you've made—recognizing triggers, using coping strategies, and prioritizing self-care. You've learned to say no when things feel overwhelming and are beginning to enjoy time with friends and family without as much anxiety.

Reflecting on your progress fills you with pride. Positive changes like better focus in school and growing confidence are showing up in your life. To celebrate, you decide to list the good things you're grateful for, and as you write, your spirits lift. Though managing anxiety and stress isn't always easy, it's worth it.

Taking time to reflect helps you appreciate the small wins, count your blessings, and find hope for the future. Every step forward is a reminder of how far you've come and all the good that lies ahead.

Your Turn

What positive changes have you noticed in your life since you started managing your anxiety and stress?

What are three things you're grateful for today?

How can reflecting on your progress make you feel more hopeful about your future?

Prayer

Dear God, thank You for helping me make progress in managing my anxiety and stress. Remind me to celebrate my accomplishments and count my blessings, no matter how small. Help me to keep growing and feeling grateful for the positive changes in my life. Amen.

53
LEARNING FROM SETBACKS

___ / ___ / _____

"For a righteous man may fall seven times and rise again."

— PROVERBS 24:16

Keira had been eagerly anticipating her journey to her dream college. She poured her heart into excelling in school, maintaining top grades, and actively participating in extracurricular activities. However, as her senior year drew to a close, life threw her an unexpected curveball—a diagnosis of a chronic illness requiring continuous treatment.

The diagnosis was a major setback for Keira. Missing school for weeks and being unable to participate in long-awaited activities left her devastated. Her parents shared her concerns about how this might derail her college aspirations. But rather than letting this challenge defeat her, Keira decided to shift her focus.

Instead of dwelling on the things she couldn't control, Keira looked at what she could still achieve. With her extra time at home, she began researching her condition, seeking ways to adapt and thrive. She connected with others who shared similar experiences, drawing strength and inspiration from their stories. Motivated to help, she started a blog to share her journey and offer encouragement to others facing similar struggles.

Keira's perseverance and optimism didn't just help her overcome her challenges—they propelled her forward. She earned her place at her dream college and even founded a support club for students with chronic illnesses.

Keira's story is a powerful reminder that setbacks don't define you. They're opportunities to learn, grow, and discover resilience you may not have known you had. Like Proverbs 24:16 says, even when life knocks you down, you have the strength to rise again.

Your Turn

Think about a time you faced a setback. How did you handle it, and what did you learn from the experience?

If you were in Keira's shoes, what steps would you take to turn a tough situation into a chance to grow?

How can you use the lessons from your setbacks to encourage others in similar situations?

Prayer

Dear God, thank You for the lessons You teach us through life's challenges. Help us to see every setback as an opportunity for growth and to trust in Your plan for us. Give us the strength and courage to rise every time we fall and to use our experiences to help others. Amen

54
EMBRACING CHANGE

___ /___ / _____

"Behold, I am doing a new thing; now it springs forth, do you not perceive it? I will make a way in the wilderness and rivers in the desert."

— ISAIAH 43:19

For as long as I can remember, I've always been an introverted and anxious person. But when I finished the managing anxiety and stress program, I started noticing positive changes in myself. I felt more confident, less anxious, and better equipped to handle challenges. These improvements gave me the courage to take steps I never thought I could before.

I began to see change not as something to fear but as an opportunity to grow and discover new aspects of myself. I decided to step out of my comfort zone by trying new things—learning to play the guitar and volunteering at a local animal shelter. While these experiences challenged me, I also found joy and fulfillment in doing them. I realized I was capable of handling situations I used to avoid, and that realization gave me the confidence to keep going.

As I reflected on my journey, I saw how much I had grown. I had learned to embrace change instead of running from it. Each new experience taught me something valuable, and with every step, I became stronger and more prepared to face the challenges life would throw my way. It's amazing to think how much we grow when we allow change to stretch and shape us.

Embracing change isn't easy, but I've learned that it's one of the most important ways to grow and develop. Rather than resisting it, I now see change as a chance to learn and discover new skills and experiences. I know I'll face challenges, but I'm also excited for the opportunities waiting for me just around the corner.

Your Turn

How have you grown or changed in the past few months?

What's something new you've tried recently, and how did it feel?

Is there a change you've been hesitant to embrace? What's holding you back?

Prayer

Dear God, thank you for helping me see change as an opportunity for growth and personal development. Give me the courage to try new things, even when I'm afraid. Help me embrace each experience as a chance to learn and grow closer to You. Thank you for walking with me on this journey and guiding me every step of the way. Amen.

55
MOVING FORWARD WITH CONFIDENCE

___ / ___ / _____

"For God gave us a spirit not of fear but of power and love and self-control."

— 2 TIMOTHY 1:7

You've recently completed an anxiety and stress management workbook that provided you with valuable tools and skills to navigate life's challenges. You've learned strategies to cope with anxiety and stress, developed self-care routines, and gained a deeper understanding of yourself. Now, as you stand at the threshold of a new chapter in your life, you can move forward with confidence, armed with the knowledge and insights you've gained.

The journey hasn't always been easy for you. There were moments when fear and self-doubt crept in, but you reminded yourself of the verse from 2 Timothy 1:7. It served as a constant reminder that you possess a spirit of power, love, and self-control—not one of fear. With this renewed perspective, you can approach each day with a sense of purpose and determination.

As you move forward, you can use the tools and skills you've learned in the anxiety and stress management workbook. Practice self-care, engage in positive self-talk, and seek support from friends and loved ones when needed. When challenges arise, you can face them head-on, knowing you have the strength within you to overcome them.

Through this journey, you've learned that moving forward with confidence means embracing the power, love, and self-control that God has gifted you. Trust in the tools and skills you've acquired and have faith in your ability to navigate life's ups and downs.

Your Turn

How has completing this anxiety and stress management workbook made a difference in your life?

In what ways can you use the tools and skills you've learned to move forward with confidence?

What are some practical ways to maintain self-care and positivity when facing new challenges?

Prayer

Dear God, thank You for guiding me through the anxiety and stress management workbook and equipping me with valuable tools and skills. As I move forward in life, help me embrace the spirit of power, love, and self-control You have given me. Grant me the wisdom to apply what I've learned and the confidence to face new challenges with grace. In Your name, Amen.

WALKING FORWARD WITH PEACE

Hey, girl—you did it! You made it to the end, and that's worth celebrating! Take a moment to give yourself a high five (or a mental one if you're in public, haha). This journey wasn't just about finishing a book—it was about stepping closer to God, learning about yourself, and finding strength for life's challenges.

I hope these devotions inspired you and reminded you of just how loved and capable you are. Life has its ups and downs, but through it all, God's got your back. He sees you, knows you, and has incredible plans for you, even if things feel uncertain right now.

If something in this book spoke to your heart or helped you, I'd love to hear about it! To do this, please leave a review on Amazon—just **scan the QR code** above or search for this book. Your words might inspire someone else to start their journey too.

Before you close this book, remember: you're a work in progress, and that's okay. God isn't asking you to have it all figured out—He just wants your heart and your trust. Every day is a new chance to grow, learn, and become the person He's calling you to be.

So, what's next? Maybe you'll re-read a favorite devotion, share it with a friend, or start journaling about what God's teaching you. Whatever it is, keep moving forward and shining your light. You're never alone —God is with you, cheering you on every step of the way.

Stay strong, stay bold, and stay YOU—because the world needs your light!

P.S. If you're looking for more encouragement or books, check out my other works on Amazon under 'Biblical Teachings.' I can't wait to see where your journey takes you next!

www.ingramcontent.com/pod-product-compliance
Lightning Source LLC
Chambersburg PA
CBHW071210070526
44584CB00019B/2979